FRENCH
SENTENCE BUILDERS

A lexicogrammar approach

Beginner to Pre-Intermediate

LISTENING
Teacher Book

Answers and Transcripts

 THE LANGUAGE GYM

Edited by Julien Barrett

 THE LANGUAGE GYM

DEDICATION

For Catrina

- Gianfranco

For Ariella and Leonard

- Dylan

For Mariana

- Ronan

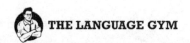

ABOUT THE AUTHORS

Gianfranco Conti taught for 25 years at schools in Italy, the UK and in Kuala Lumpur, Malaysia. He has also been a university lecturer, holds a Master's degree in Applied Linguistics and a PhD in metacognitive strategies as applied to second language writing. He is now an author, a popular independent educational consultant and professional development provider. He has written around 2,000 resources for the TES website, which have awarded him the Best Resources Contributor in 2015. He has co-authored the best-selling and influential book for world languages teachers, "The Language Teacher Toolkit" and "Breaking the sound barrier: Teaching learners how to listen", in which he puts forth his Listening As Modelling methodology. Gianfranco writes an influential blog on second language acquisition called The Language Gym, co-founded the interactive website language-gym.com and the Facebook professional group Global Innovative Language Teachers (GILT). Last but not least, Gianfranco has created the instructional approach known as E.P.I. (Extensive Processing Instruction).

Dylan Viñales has taught for 15 years, in schools in Bath, Beijing and Kuala Lumpur in state, independent and international settings. He lives in Kuala Lumpur. He is fluent in five languages, and gets by in several more. Dylan is, besides a teacher, a professional development provider, specialising in E.P.I., metacognition, teaching languages through music (especially ukulele) and cognitive science. In the last five years, together with Dr Conti, he has driven the implementation of E.P.I. in one of the top international schools in the world: Garden International School. This has allowed him to test, on a daily basis, the sequences and activities included in this book with excellent results (his students have won language competitions both locally and internationally). He has designed an original Spanish curriculum, bespoke instructional materials, based on Reading and Listening as Modelling (RAM and LAM). Dylan co-founded the fastest growing professional development group for modern languages teachers on Facebook, Global Innovative Languages Teachers, which includes over 12,000 teachers from all corners of the globe. He authors an influential blog on modern language pedagogy in which he supports the teaching of languages through E.P.I. Dylan is the lead author of Spanish content on the Language Gym website and oversees the technological development of the site. He is currently undertaking the NPQML qualification, after which he plans to pursue a Masters in second language acquisition.

Ronan Jézéquel has taught for 15 years, in schools in Frimley, Brighton and Kuala Lumpur in state and international settings. He lives in Kuala Lumpur. He is fluent in three languages, and gets by in several more. Ronan is, besides a teacher, a keen mountain biker and an outdoor enthusiast. In the last five years, together with Dr Conti and Dylan Viñales, he has contributed to the implementation of E.P.I. in one of the top international schools in the world: Garden International School. This has allowed him to test, on a daily basis, the sequences and activities included in this book with excellent results. Ronan is the lead author of French content on The Language Gym website and he also brings the competitive element from his sporty background to TLG with the design of live games and features such as our leaderboard.

ACKNOWLEDGEMENTS

Many thanks to the native speakers who contributed to the recording process. In particular, thanks to Julien Barrett, Sophie Barré, Alexia Barton, Julie Das and Sophie Youill for their time and effort in recording the sound files.

Secondly, our thanks and appreciation to the testing and proofreading team, Julien Barrett & Sophie Barré. It is thanks to their time, patience and professionalism that we have been able to produce a refined and highly accurate product.

 **THE LANGUAGE GYM**

EXTENSIVE PROCESSING INSTRUCTION

If you have bought into our E.P.I. approach

Both this listening book and the original Sentence Builder book were originally designed as a resource to use in conjunction with our E.P.I. approach and teaching strategies. Our course favours flooding comprehensible input, organising content by communicative functions and related constructions, and a big focus on reading and listening as modelling. The aim of these books is to empower the beginner-to-pre-intermediate learner with linguistic tools - high-frequency structures and vocabulary - useful for real-life communication.

If you don't know or have NOT yet bought into our approach

If you would like to learn about E.P.I. you could read one of the authors' blogs. The definitive guide is Dr Conti's "Patterns First – How I Teach Lexicogrammar" which can be found on his blog (www.gianfrancoconti.com). There are also informative and user-friendly blogs on Dylan's Wordpress site (mrvinalesmfl.wordpress.com) such as "Using sentence builders to reduce (everyone's) workload and create more fluent linguists" which can be read to get teaching ideas and to learn how to structure a course, through all the stages of E.P.I.

The book "Breaking the Sound Barrier: Teaching Learners how to Listen" by Gianfranco Conti and Steve Smith, provides a detailed description of the approach and of the listening and speaking activities you can use in synergy with the present book.

INTRODUCTION

This French Listening Booklet matches to the minutest details the content of the 19 units included in the best-selling workbook for beginner-to-pre-intermediate learners "French sentence builders", by the same authors. For best results, the two books should be used together.

This book fully implements Dr Conti's popular approach to listening-skills instruction, L.A.M. (aka *Listening-As-Modelling*), laid out in his seminal work: "Breaking the Sound Barrier: Teaching Learners how to Listen" (Conti and Smith, 2019). L.A.M. is based on the concept that listening instruction should train students in the mastery of the key micro-listening skills identified by cognitive psychologists as follows:

- Phonemic processing

- Syllable processing

- Segmenting

- Lexical retrieval

- Parsing

- Meaning building

- Discourse building

This translates into aural instruction which deliberately targets the above micro-abilities through a range of tasks performed on input which is (1) highly patterned; (2) 90-98 % comprehensible; (3) flooded with the occurrence of the target structural patterns and lexical items; (4) delivered at a rate of speed which allows for learning; (5) designed to induce a priming effect on learning (i.e. to subconsciously sensitize the learners to the target language items).

Each unit contains around 13 listening tasks, which provide continuous and extensive recycling of the target constructions and vocabulary items and address the development of the key listening micro-skills. The tasks include engaging and tested Conti classics such as "Spot the intruder", "Missing details", "Faulty transcript", "Break the flow", "Faulty translation", "Gapped translation" and "Listening slalom", alongside more traditional listening comprehension tasks.

The tasks have been designed with the following key L.A.M. principles in mind: (1) the task's cognitive load must be appropriate to the level of the target learners; (2) the tasks must involve thorough processing (i.e. they should promote attention to details); (3) at the beginning stages, the tasks should promote noticing of the target language items by creating opportunities for cognitive comparison between the target language and the mother tongue (e.g. by using parallel texts in both languages, as happens in tasks such as "Bad translation" and "Gapped translation"); (4) the tasks should provide the learners with multiple entry points for acquisition by requiring them to engage with the same or similar texts at different levels of processing (from the identification of sounds to lexical retrieval; from the processing of structural patterns to the construction of meaning and discourse); (5) the tasks should model speaking micro-skills (e.g. pronunciation, decoding skills, functional and positional processing), not merely exam-taking techniques (as textbooks typically do); (6) tasks should be sequenced in a graded fashion, gradually phasing out support and increasing in difficulty.

The tasks have been tested countless times with students aged 11 to 13, with very positive feedback both in terms of engagement and perceived effectiveness. In particular, Dylan and Ronan have been pioneers of the approach and used it exclusively, and extensively, over the last 4 years at Garden International School, with excellent results in terms of both student engagement and progress.

HOW TO USE THIS BOOK

This book was intended as a Listening-for-learning tool aimed at paving the way for spoken and/or written production. If used in conjunction with the "French Sentence Builders" book, the tasks in each unit would follow the presentational stage of the target constructions through sentence builders and associated teacher-led aural activities aimed at building phonological awareness (e.g. "Faulty echo", "Minimal pairs", "Spot the silent letters", "Write it as you hear it") and at establishing meaning (e.g. "Listening bingo", "Positive or Negative", "Faulty transcript").

We recommend interspersing the listening tasks in each unit with engaging vocabulary-building, reading and read-aloud activities rather than covering every single exercise in a sequential fashion. Also, teachers, in selecting the activities and crafting each instructional sequence, should be cognizant of the motivational levels and concentration span of their students. These will vary from class to class and will inevitably inform their choice of the amount and type of listening that will be most conducive to learning.

Please note that whilst the sequence in which the tasks are arranged in each unit was carefully crafted by the authors to provide a graded and balanced progression from easier to more challenging, teachers should not feel straight-jacketed by that order.

If the teacher has near native or native command of the target language, they may want to deliver some of activities by reading the text aloud themselves using the transcripts provided in the accompanying teacher book (bought separately). This will enable them to enhance the input by emphasizing specific aspects of the input (e.g. specific words, word endings or phonotactic features such as assimilation phenomena) they may want their students to notice. Input enhancement is a useful means to enhance acquisition and interpersonal listening whereby the teacher interacts with the learners is an effective way to make aural input more learnable, engaging and motivational.

ACCESSING THE SOUND FILES

The sound files can be accessed at www.language-gym.com/listening (password is "**penguin**").

Once you log on, you will see a menu, containing all the units in the book, ordered and labelled as per the book itself.

IMPORTANT NOTICE: Please note, that this section of the Language Gym can be accessed by any person who has bought this book, regardless of whether or not you are a subscriber to the main Language Gym site. Under no circumstances should this password be shared with a teacher, **outside of your school**, who has not bought the book. This extends to other schools inside a collective of schools, such as a trust. In brief: every school should buy their own book. The book should not be shared outside of your school.

CHOOSING A DIFFICULTY LEVEL

Please note that several activities contain a normal and a "faster" version. These have been added in as a differentiation tool. It is up to the individual teacher's discretion which file to use, based on their knowledge of the students in their classes.

 THE LANGUAGE GYM

TABLE OF CONTENTS

Unit	Title	Communicative function	Page
1	Talking about my age	Describing yourself and other people	1
2	Saying when my birthday is	Describing yourself and other people	3
3	Describing hair and eyes	Describing yourself and other people	6
4	Saying where I live and am from	Indicating location	9
5	Talking about my family members (age and relationships)	Describing people and relationships	12
6	Describing myself and another family member	Describing people, relationships and expressing opinions	15
7	Talking about pets	Describing people/animals and asking questions	18
8	Talking about jobs	Describing people, expressing opinions and indicating location	21
9	Comparing people's appearance and personality	Comparing and contrasting	24
10	Saying what's in my school bag / classroom	Stating what you have and describing objects	27
11	Talking about food - Introduction	Describing food and expressing opinions	30
12	Talking about food - Likes / dislikes	Describing routine behaviour in the present, expressing opinions	33
13	Talking about clothes and accessories	Describing people, routine behaviour in the present and indicating time	36
14	Saying what I and others do in our free time	Describing routine behaviour in the present and indicating time	39
15	Talking about weather and free time	Describing events and routine behaviour in the present and indicating location	42
16	Talking about my daily routine	Describing routine behaviour in the present, indicating time, sequencing	45
17	Describing my house	Indicating location, describing things and expressing likes/dislikes	48
18	Saying what I do at home / daily routine	Indicating routine behaviour in the present, time, frequency and location	51
19	Talking about future plans and holidays	Making plans for the future, indicating time, location and expressing opinions	54

UNIT 1 – TALKING ABOUT MY AGE

1. Complete the gaps

a. Je m'**appelle** Alexandre.
b. J'ai **quinze** ans.
c. J'ai **deux** frères.
d. **Mon** frère aîné s'**appelle** Robert.
e. Mon **frère** cadet s'appelle Julien.
f. Comment tu **t'**appelles?
g. Quel **âge** as-tu?

2. Break the flow

a. Je m'appelle Anthony et j'ai douze ans.
b. J'ai quinze ans.
c. Mon frère s'appelle Pierre.
d. Ma sœur s'appelle Anne.
e. Quel âge as-tu?
f. Mon frère s'appelle Philippe.
g. Comment tu t'appelles?

3. Arrange in the order in which you hear

I am thirteen years old.	2
Anne is fifteen years old.	7
My name is Paul.	1
My sister is called Anne.	5
I have a brother and a sister.	3
My brother is called Fernand.	4
Fernand is seventeen years old.	6

TRANSCRIPT: Je m'appelle Paul. J'ai treize ans. J'ai un frère et une sœur. Mon frère s'appelle Fernand. Ma sœur s'appelle Anne. Fernand a dix-sept ans. Anne a quinze ans.

4. Spot the differences and correct your text

a. Je m'appelle **Marina**.

b. J'ai **douze** ans.

c. J'ai deux **frères**.

d. Mon frère aîné s'appelle **Paul**.

e. Mon frère **cadet** s'appelle Robert.

f. Paul a **quinze** ans.

g. Robert a **neuf** ans.

h. Quel âge **as-tu?**

5. Faulty translation: spot the nine translation errors and correct them

a. **MY** name is Émilie.
b. I am **FRENCH**.
c. I have three **SISTERS**.
d. My **YOUNGER** sister is called Mélanie.
e. My **OLDER** sister is called **LÉA**.
f. Mélanie is **11**.
g. Léa is **13**.
h. Me, I am **12**.

TRANSCRIPT:

a. Je m'appelle Émilie.
b. Je suis française.
c. J'ai trois sœurs.
d. Ma sœur cadette s'appelle Mélanie.
e. Ma sœur aînée s'appelle Léa.
f. Mélanie a onze ans.
g. Léa a treize ans.
h. Moi, j'ai douze ans.

6. Spot and write in the seven missing words

a. **(Bonjour)**, je m'appelle Pierre.

b. Je viens **(de)** France.

c. J'ai treize **(ans)**.

d. J'ai un frère **(et)** une sœur.

e. Mon frère **(s')** appelle Robert.

f. **(Ma)** sœur s'appelle Isabelle.

g. Robert **(a)** quatorze ans.

 THE LANGUAGE GYM

7. Spot the error in the sentences below: listen and correct

a. J'**ai** quatorze ans.

b. Je **m'**appelle Charles.

c. Mon frère s'appelle **Paul**.

d. J'ai **deux** frères.

e. J'ai **un** frère et une sœur.

f. Quel âge **as-tu**?

9. Complete with the missing letters

a. Je **M**appelle Pierre

b. Je suis d**U** Pays basque.

c. J'ai quin**Z**e ans.

d. Je n'ai p**A**s de frère.

e. Mais j'ai un**E** sœur.

f. Ma soeur **S**'appelle Anne.

g. Alice a do**U**ze a**N**s.

h. Et toi, comment tu **T**'appelles?

i. Quel âge as-t**U**?

11. Narrow listening one: gap-fill

Je m'appelle **ANTHONY**. Je suis de Quimper, en **FRANCE**. Dans ma famille, il y a cinq personnes: **MA** mère, mon père, mes **DEUX** frères et moi. Mon frère **AÎNÉ** s'appelle Michel et mon frère **CADET** s'appelle Paul. Michel a **QUINZE** ans et mon frère Paul a **SIX** ans. Et toi, comment tu t'**APPELLES**? Quel âge as-tu?

appelles	Anthony	cadet	ma	six
aîné	quinze	France	quel	deux

8. Listen and fill in the grid

		Age	Brothers	Sisters
1	Marie	12	2	0
2	Joël	14	4	1
2	Paul	8	1	1
4	Anne	11	0	0
5	Émilie	5	2	2
6	Mélanie	15	0	3

TRANSCRIPT: (1) Je m'appelle Marie et j'ai douze ans. J'ai deux frères, mais je n'ai pas de sœurs. **(2)** Je m'appelle Joël et j'ai quatorze ans. J'ai quatre frères et une sœur. **(3)** Je m'appelle Paul et j'ai huit ans. J'ai un frère et une sœur. **(4)** Je m'appelle Anne et j'ai onze ans. Je suis fille unique. Je n'ai ni de frère, ni de sœur. **(5)** Je m'appelle Émilie et j'ai cinq ans. J'ai deux frères et deux sœurs. **(6)** Je m'appelle Mélanie et j'ai quinze ans. J'ai trois sœurs, mais pas de frères.

10. Translate the nine sentences you hear into English

a. I am called Robert.

b. I am 14.

c. I have an older and a younger brother.

d. My older brother is called Émilien.

e. My younger brother is called Éric.

f. Émilien is 15 years old.

g. Éric is 12 years old.

h. And you, what is your name?

i. How old are you?

TRANSCRIPT: (a) Je m'appelle Robert. **(b)** J'ai quatorze ans. **(c)** J'ai un frère aîné et un frère cadet. **(d)** Mon frère aîné s'appelle Émilien. **(e)** Mon frère cadet s'appelle Éric. **(f)** Emilien a quinze ans. **(g)** Éric a douze ans. **(h)** Et toi, comment tu t'appelles? **(i)** Quel âge as-tu?

12. Narrow listening two: gapped translation

ANSWERS: (1) Sylvie **(2)** Marseille **(3)** 5 **(4)** Younger **(5)** Older **(6)** Older **(7)** Sébastien **(8)** 14 **(9)** Younger **(10)** 7 **(11)** What is your name? **(12)** How old are you? **(13)** How many brothers and sisters do you have?

TRANSCRIPT: Je m'appelle **Sylvie**. Je suis de **Marseille** en France. Dans ma famille, il y a **cinq** personnes: ma mère, mon père, mon frère **cadet**, mon frère **aîné** et moi. Mon frère **aîné** s'appelle **Sébastien**. Il a **quatorze** ans. Mon frère **cadet** s'appelle Anthony. Il a **sept** ans.

Et toi, **comment tu t'appelles? Quel âge as-tu? Combien de frères et sœurs as-tu?**

UNIT 2 – SAYING WHEN MY BIRTHDAY IS

1. Complete

a. Je m'**appelle** Alexandre et mon anniversaire est **le** quinze **mai**.

b. **Je** m'appelle Pierre et **mon** anniversaire **est** le deux **mars**.

c. Je m'appelle **Martine** et mon anniversaire est **le** trois **juin**.

d. **Je** suis Léo et mon anniversaire est le **six septembre**.

e. **Je** m'**appelle** Paul et mon anniversaire **est** le **vingt** décembre.

2. Break the flow

a. Mon anniversaire est le treize octobre.

b. Mon anniversaire est le neuf mai.

c. Quelle est la date de ton anniversaire?

d. Mon anniversaire est le premier août.

e. Mon anniversaire est le seize juillet.

f. Quelle est la date de son anniversaire?

g. Mon frère a quatorze ans.

h. Son anniversaire est le deux janvier.

i. Quelle est la date de l'anniversaire de ton amie?

3. Arrange in the order in which you hear

Salut, je m'appelle Fernand.	1
J'ai un frère.	6
Je suis allemand.	2
Son anniversaire est le cinq mars.	7
Mais j'habite à Paris.	3
J'ai dix ans.	4
Mon anniversaire est le treize juillet.	5

4. Spot the nine differences and correct your text

a. Je m'appelle **Georges**.

b. Je n'ai pas de **sœurs**.

c. Je suis **fils** unique.

d. Je viens de la **Martinique**.

e. Mais j'habite en **Angleterre**.

f. J'ai **cinq** ans.

g. Mon anniversaire est le quatorze **juillet**.

h. Ma **meilleure** amie, Louise, a treize ans.

i. Son anniversaire est le **huit** octobre.

5. Faulty translation: spot the ten translation errors and correct them

a. My name is Robert and I am eleven years old. My birthday is on 4th of **June**.

b. My mother's name is Alice. She is **27** years old. Her birthday on **14th** August.

c. My father's name is Périg. He is 39 years old. His birthday is on **18th** January.

d. I have three **sisters**.

e. My brother Alex is **14** and his birthday is on **7th** July.

f. My brother Nico is **19** and his birthday is on 22nd **March**.

g. Do you have any **sisters**?

TRANSCRIPT:

(a) Je m'appelle Robert et j'ai 11 ans. Mon anniversaire est le 4 juin. **(b)** Ma mère s'appelle Alice. Elle a 27 ans. Son anniversaire est le 14 août. **(c)** Mon père s'appelle Périg. Il a 39 ans. Son anniversaire est le 18 janvier. **(d)** J'ai trois sœurs. **(e)** Mon frère Alex a 14 ans et son anniversaire est le sept juillet. **(f)** Mon frère Nico a 19 ans et son anniversaire est le 22 mars. **(g)** Tu as des sœurs?

6. Spot and write in the nine missing details

Je m'appelle Robert, je suis français **et** je vis en Allemagne. J'ai douze **ans**. Dans ma famille, il y a cinq **personnes**: mon père, ma mère et **mes** deux frères. Mon frère aîné **s'appelle** Pierre et **mon** frère cadet s'appelle Romuald. Pierre a quinze ans et **son** anniversaire est **le** douze avril. Romuald a neuf ans et son anniversaire est **le** vingt juillet.

7. Spot the errors in the sentences below: listen and correct

a. Mon anniversaire **est** le vingt juin.
b. Mon amie s'appelle Patricia. **Elle** a dix ans et son anniversaire est le quinze mai.
c. L'anniversaire de mon amie est **le** neuf avril.
d. Ma mère **a** trente-huit ans et son **anniversaire** est le trente novembre.
e. Mon ami **s'**appelle Robert. Son anniversaire est le quatorze **octobre**.

9. Complete with the missing letters

a. Je m'appelle Serge.
b. Je n'ai pas de f**r**ères.
c. Je suis fils **u**nique.
d. Je su**i**s du Portugal.
e. Mais j'h**a**bite en Italie.
f. J'ai quin**z**e ans.
g. Mon anniversaire est le quatorze **j**uin.
h. Ma p**e**tite amie, Carmen, a treize ans.
i. Son anniversaire est le dix-hu**i**t octobre.

8. Listen and fill in the grid ANSWERS

		Country	Age	Birthday
1	Alex	La Réunion	12	3.06
2	Paul	Portugal	15	17.07
3	Nina	Espagne	9	12.11
4	Dylan	Gibraltar	5	7.06
5	Michel	Écosse	16	20.09
6	Martine	Martinique	14	14.12

TRANSCRIPT
(1) Salut, je m'appelle Alex et je suis de la Réunion. J'ai 12 ans et mon anniversaire est le 3 juin.
(2) Bonjour, je m'appelle Paul et je suis du Portugal. J'ai 15 ans et mon anniversaire est le 17 juillet.
(3) Salut, je m'appelle Nina et je viens d'Espagne. J'ai 9 ans et mon anniversaire est le 12 novembre.
(4) Salut, je m'appelle Dylan et je viens de Gibraltar. J'ai 5 ans et mon anniversaire est le 7 juin.
(5) Bonjour, je m'appelle Michel et je suis d'Écosse. J'ai 16 ans et mon anniversaire est le 20 septembre.
(6) Salut, je m'appelle Martine et je suis de la Martinique. J'ai 14 ans et mon anniversaire est le 14 décembre.

10. Translate the ten sentences you hear into English TRANSCRIPT:

a. Je m'appelle Carmen.
b. J'ai quinze ans.
c. Mon anniversaire est le premier janvier.
d. J'ai deux sœurs.
e. Ma sœur aînée s'appelle Béatrice.
f. Elle a dix-sept ans.
g. Son anniversaire est le quatorze juillet.
h. Ma sœur cadette s'appelle Hélène.
i. Hélène a douze ans.
j. Son anniversaire est le dix novembre.

10. Translate the ten sentences you hear into English ANSWERS:

a. My name is Carmen.
b. I am 15 years old.
c. My birthday is on the 1st January.
d. I have two sisters.
e. My older sister is called Béatrice.
f. She is 17 years old.
g. Her birthday is on the 14th July.
h. My younger sister is called Hélène.
i. Hélène is 12 years old.
j. Her birthday is on the 10th November.

11. Narrow listening one: gap-fill

Salut, je m'appelle Sylvie et je **suis** de Biarritz, en France. J'ai **14** ans. Mon anniversaire est le **30** mai, j'ai deux frères, Philippe et Gérard. Philippe **a** quatorze ans et son anniversaire est le vingt-et-un **mars**. Mon frère Gérard a seize ans et **son** anniversaire est le **20** juin. À la **maison** nous avons aussi un hamster. Il s'**appelle** Joli et a deux ans. Ma meilleure **amie** s'appelle Magalie. Elle a **15** ans. Son anniversaire est le **12** janvier.

12. Narrow listening two: fill in the grid in English

Name	Georges
Town	Grenoble
Age	18
Birthday	20.06
Brother's age	15
Brother's birthday	12.01

TRANSCRIPT:
Salut, je m'appelle Georges et je suis de Grenoble. J'ai dix-huit ans et mon anniversaire est le vingt juin. Mon frère a quinze ans et son anniversaire est le douze janvier.

13. Narrow listening three: gapped translation

ANSWERS: My name is **Arielle**. I am **14** years old. I am from **Valence**, in **France**. My birthday is on **16**[th] **July**. I have a **brother** called **Jérôme**. **He** is **11** years old. **His** birthday is on **13**[th] **December**. My best friend is called **Anne**. She is **15** years old and her birthday is on **10**[th] **March**. My cousin is called **Nicole**. She is **12** years old and her birthday is on **1**[st] **April**. At home, we have a pet. It is a **snake**. Its name is **Cobra** and is **3** years old.

TRANSCRIPT: Je m'appelle Arielle. J'ai quatorze ans. Je suis de Valence, en France. Mon anniversaire est le seize juillet. J'ai un frère qui s'appelle Jérôme. Il a onze ans. Son anniversaire est le treize décembre. Ma meilleure amie s'appelle Anne. Elle a quinze ans et son anniversaire est le 10 mars. Ma cousine s'appelle Nicole. Elle a douze ans et son anniversaire est le premier avril. À la maison, nous avons un animal. C'est un serpent. Il s'appelle Cobra et a trois ans.

---

14. Listening slalom: write the correct numbers (#1 is done as an example)

1	2	3	4	5
My name is Andréa (1)	My brother is called Léon (2)	My name is Alexandre (3)	My name is Gabrièle (4)	My name is Charles (5)
I am from Valence (5)	**I am from Calais (1)**	I am from Bayonne (4)	He is from Saint-Étienne (2)	I am from Grenoble (3)
He is 14 (2)	I am 21 (3)	**I am 13 (1)**	I am 9 (5)	I am 16 (4)
His birthday is on 15th March (2)	**My birthday is on 16th July (1)**	My birthday is on 21st May (4)	My birthday is on 23rd June (5)	My birthday is on 30th August (3)
I have a girlfriend (5)	I have a hamster (3)	I have a boyfriend (4)	He has a girlfriend (2)	**I have a sister (1)**
His birthday is on 12th (4)	Her birthday is on 7th (2)	**Her birthday is on 1st (1)**	His birthday is on 2nd (3)	Her birthday is on 30th (5)
January (1)	March (4)	October (2)	June (5)	September (3)

TRANSCRIPT:

(1) Exemple: Je m'appelle Andréa. Je suis de Calais. J'ai treize ans et mon anniversaire est le 16 juillet. J'ai une sœur. Son anniversaire est le premier janvier.

(2) Mon frère s'appelle Léon. Il est de Saint-Étienne. Il a quatorze ans. Son anniversaire est le 15 mars. Il a une petite amie. Son anniversaire est le sept octobre.

(3) Je m'appelle Alexandre. Je suis de Grenoble. J'ai vingt-et-un ans. Mon anniversaire est le 30 août. J'ai un hamster. Son anniversaire est le 2 septembre.

(4) Je m'appelle Gabrièle. Je suis de Bayonne. J'ai seize ans. Mon anniversaire est le 21 mai. J'ai un petit ami. Son anniversaire est le 12 mars.

(5) Je m'appelle Charles. Je suis de Valence. J'ai neuf ans. Mon anniversaire est le 23 juin. J'ai une petite amie. Son anniversaire est le 30 juin.

---

15. Faulty translation: spot and correct the mistakes found in the translation

ANSWERS: My name is Marc and I am from **France**. I am **12** years old. My parents are called Alain and Marina. They are **48** years old. My mother's birthday is on 21st March. My father's birthday is on **14**[th] August. I have two **brothers**, Raphaël and Anthony. Raphaël is 10 years old, and Anthony is **11**. Raphaël's birthday is on 11th **June**. Anthony's birthday in on 21st April. At home we have a pet, a **cat**. Its name is Pacotille, it's 1 year old. I have a girlfriend. Her name is Patricia. She is **13**. Her birthday is on 16th **November**.

TRANSCRIPT: Je m'appelle Marc et je suis de **France**. J'ai 12 ans. Mes parents s'appellent Alain et Marina. Ils ont **48** ans. L'anniversaire de ma mère est le 21 mars. L'anniversaire de mon père est le **14** août. J'ai deux **frères**, Raphaël et Anthony. Raphaël a 10 ans, et Anthony a **11** ans. L'anniversaire de Raphaël est le 11 **juin**. L'anniversaire d'Anthony est le 21 avril. A la maison, nous avons un animal: un **chat**. Il s'appelle Pacotille, et il a 1 an. J'ai une petite amie. Elle s'appelle Patricia. Elle a **13** ans. Son anniversaire est le 16 **novembre**.

UNIT 3 – DESCRIBING HAIR AND EYES

1. Complete

a. J'ai **les** cheveux **roux**.

b. Mon frère **a** les cheveux **noirs**.

c. J'ai **les** yeux **bleus**.

d. Anthony **a** les **cheveux** blonds et les yeux **verts**.

e. **Ma** sœur **porte** des lunettes.

f. J'ai **les cheveux** courts et en **épis**.

g. J'ai les **yeux** marron et **j'ai** une barbe.

2. Break the flow

a. J'ai les cheveux noirs et raides.

b. Il a de grands yeux bleus.

c. Elle a les cheveux noirs et mi-longs.

d. Il a les cheveux châtains, longs et frisés.

e. Je n'ai pas de cheveux.

f. Elle a les yeux noirs, et elle porte des lunettes.

g. Tu as les yeux marron et tu as une moustache.

3. Arrange in the order in which you hear

Je m'appelle François.	1
J'ai douze ans.	3
Mon anniversaire est le trente mars.	4
J'ai les cheveux noirs, raides et courts.	6
Je suis de Valence en France.	2
Il a les cheveux blonds et les yeux verts.	10
Il a quinze ans.	8
Son anniversaire est le quatorze mars.	9
J'ai un frère.	7
J'ai les yeux noirs.	5

4. Spot the intruders: identify the word in each sentence the speaker is not saying

a. J'ai les cheveux **très** longs.

b. Elle a les cheveux **mi-**longs.

c. Mon père a les cheveux **assez** courts.

d. Ma mère **n'a pas** les cheveux longs.

e. Mon frère **cadet** a les cheveux blonds.

f. Ma sœur a les cheveux **noirs** en épis.

5. Spot the differences between the recording and the text: correct the sentences

a. Je m'appelle **Sylvie**.

b. J'ai **dix-sept** ans.

c. Je viens d'**Allemagne**.

d. …mais j'habite en **Irlande**.

e. J'ai les cheveux **noirs** et les yeux marron.

f. J'ai les cheveux longs et **frisés**.

g. Ma meilleure amie, Catherine, a **quinze** ans.

h. Elle est belle. Elle a les cheveux blonds, très longs et **ondulés**.

i. Elle a les yeux **bleus** et elle porte des lunettes.

6. Complete

a. J'ai les cheveux en ép**is**.

b. J'ai les cheveux chât**ains**.

c. J'ai les yeux no**irs**.

d. J'ai les cheveux lo**ngs**.

e. J'ai les yeux bl**eus**.

f. Je ne porte pas de lu**nettes**.

g. Je n'ai pas de mou**stache**.

h. J'ai une bar**be**.

i. Mon père **a** une moustache.

j. Mon frère a les yeux gr**is**.

THE LANGUAGE GYM

6

7. Faulty translation: spot and correct the ten translation errors

ANSWERS: (a) My name is Charles. I am **fifteen** years old. **(b)** My birthday is on 14ᵗʰ **July**. **(c)** I have **three** brothers. **(d)** I have black hair, **short** and curly. **(e)** I have **green** eyes and I wear glasses. **(f)** My older brother is called Paul. He is **nineteen**. **(g)** His birthday is on 20ᵗʰ **June**. **(h)** He has blond hair, short and **straight**. **(i)** He has **grey** eyes, and he wears glasses. **(j)** He has a **beard**.

TRANSCRIPT:
a. Je m'appelle Charles. J'ai quinze ans.
b. Mon anniversaire est le 14 juillet.
c. J'ai trois frères.
d. J'ai les cheveux noirs, courts et frisés.
e. J'ai les yeux verts et je porte des lunettes.
f. Mon frère aîné s'appelle Paul. Il a dix-neuf ans.
g. Son anniversaire est le 20 juin.
h. Il a les cheveux blonds, courts et raides.
i. Il a les yeux gris, et il porte des lunettes.
j. Il a une barbe.

8. Spot the nine missing words and write them in

Je m'appelle Jean-Michel. J'ai **les** cheveux blonds, longs **et** frisés et les yeux bleus. Ma mère s'appelle Martine et mon père **s'appelle** Claude. Ma mère a les cheveux noirs, très longs et ondulés et **les** yeux marron. Mon père est complètement **chauve** et il a les yeux verts. J'ai un frère **qui** s'appelle Fernand. Il **a** les cheveux blonds, courts et frisés et les yeux bleus. Fernand porte des lunettes. J'ai aussi une **petite** amie qui s'appelle Patricia. Elle a les cheveux roux, **mi**-longs et raides. Elle a les yeux verts.

9. Spot the errors in the sentences below: listen and correct

TRANSCRIPT:
a. Je **m'appelle** Michel.
b. J'ai **treize** ans.
c. J'ai **les** cheveux noirs, longs et raides.
d. J'ai **les** yeux bleus.
e. Je porte **des** lunettes.
f. Mon frère **s'appelle** Paul.
g. J'ai **quatorze** ans.
h. Paul **a** les cheveux blonds, courts et frisés.
i. Il a les yeux noirs. Il ne porte pas **de** lunettes.

10. Listen and fill in the grid

	Hair	Eyes	Wears glasses
Joël	Red	Blue	Yes
Paul	Light brown	Grey	No
Nina	Brown	Green	No
Dylan	Blond	Blue	Yes
Michel	Red	Brown	Yes
Marie	Black	Grey	No

10. Listen and fill in the grid

TRANSCRIPT:

Je m'appelle **Joël**. J'ai les cheveux roux et les yeux bleus. Je porte des lunettes.

Je m'appelle **Paul**. J'ai les cheveux châtains et les yeux gris. Je ne porte pas de lunettes.

Je m'appelle **Nina** et j'ai les cheveux bruns et les yeux verts. Je ne porte pas de lunettes.

Je m'appelle **Dylan**. J'ai les cheveux blonds et les yeux bleus. Je porte des lunettes.

Je m'appelle **Michel**. J'ai les cheveux roux et les yeux marron. Je porte des lunettes.

Je m'appelle **Marie**. J'ai les cheveux noirs et les yeux gris. Je ne porte pas de lunettes.

11. Translate the ten sentences you hear into English
ANSWERS:
a. I have light brown hair.
b. My mother has blond hair.
c. My father has black hair.
d. My brother has red hair.
e. My sister has black hair.
f. I have curly hair.
g. My mother has straight hair.
h. My father has long hair.
i. My brother has wavy hair.
j. My sister has medium length hair.

TRANSCRIPT:
a. J'ai les cheveux châtains.
b. Ma mère a les cheveux blonds.
c. Mon père a les cheveux noirs.
d. Mon frère a les cheveux roux.
e. Ma sœur a les cheveux noirs.
f. J'ai les cheveux frisés.
g. Ma mère a les cheveux raides.
h. Mon père a les cheveux longs.
i. Mon frère a les cheveux ondulés.
j. Ma sœur a les cheveux mi-longs.

 **THE LANGUAGE GYM**

12. Narrow listening three: gapped translation

ANSWERS: My name is Véronique, I am **15** years old. My birthday is on the **12** of **January**. In my family there are **5** people: my father, my mother and my two **sisters**. My mother has **light brown** hair, **long** and curly. She has **blue** eyes. My father has grey hair, **short** and straight. He has **brown** eyes. My two sisters have **blond** hair, long and straight. They both have **green** eyes. I have light brown **very short** hair. However, before, I used to have **long** hair.

TRANSCRIPT: Je m'appelle Véronique, j'ai **15** ans. Mon anniversaire est le **12 janvier**. Dans ma famille, il y a **5** personnes: mon père, ma mère et mes deux **sœurs**. Ma mère a les cheveux **châtains**, **longs** et frisés. Elle a les yeux **bleus**. Mon père a les cheveux gris, **courts** et raides. Il a les yeux **marron.** Mes deux sœurs ont les cheveux **blonds**, longs et raides. Elles ont toutes les deux les yeux **verts**. Moi, j'ai les cheveux châtains **très courts**. Cependant, avant, j'avais les cheveux **longs**.

13. Listening slalom: write the correct numbers (#1 is done as an example)

1	2	3	4	5
My name is Marcel (1)	My name is Alice (2)	My name is Magalie (3)	My name is Kevin (4)	My name is Jean-Claude (5)
I am from Valence (4)	**I am from Brussels (1)**	I am from Bayonne (5)	I am from Saint-Étienne (2)	I am from Grenoble (3)
but I live in Rome, Italy (3)	but I live in Paris (4)	but I live in Dakar, Sénégal (2)	**but I live in London, UK (1)**	but I live in Madrid, Spain (5)
I have one brother (4)	I have two brothers (2)	**I am only child (1)**	I have one sister (5)	I have one brother and one sister (3)
I have blond hair (3)	I have brown hair (4)	I have red hair (5)	I have black hair (2)	**I have light brown hair (1)**
long and straight (5)	short and spiky (2)	**long and curly (1)**	short and wavy (4)	medium length and straight (3)
I have blue eyes (1)	I have brown eyes (5)	I have green eyes (2)	I have grey eyes (3)	I have blue eyes (4)

TRANSCRIPT:

(1) Exemple: Je m'appelle Marcel. Je suis de Bruxelles, mais je vis à Londres en Angleterre. Je suis fils unique et j'ai les cheveux châtains, longs et frisés. J'ai les yeux bleus.

(2) Je m'appelle Alice. Je suis de Saint-Étienne, mais j'habite à Dakar au Sénégal. J'ai deux frères. J'ai les cheveux noirs, courts et en épis. J'ai les yeux verts.

(3) Je m'appelle Magalie. Je suis de Grenoble, mais je vis à Rome en Italie. J'ai un frère et une sœur. J'ai les cheveux blonds, mi-longs et raides. J'ai les yeux gris.

(4) Je m'appelle Kevin. Je suis de Valence, mais j'habite à Paris. J'ai un frère. J'ai les cheveux bruns, courts et ondulés. J'ai les yeux bleus.

(5) Je m'appelle Jean-Claude. Je suis de Bayonne, mais j'habite à Madrid en Espagne. J'ai une sœur. J'ai les cheveux roux, longs et raides. J'ai les yeux marron.

14. Fill in the grid

1. Matéo: Example **2. Philippe:** 15, one sister, green **3. André:** 15th January, light brown, short, straight hair
4. Éric: 10, three sisters, brown eyes **5. Mélanie:** 25th December, red, short and straight hair
6. Alain: 14, only child, grey eyes

TRANSCRIPT: (1) Je m'appelle Matéo. J'ai 12 ans et mon anniversaire est le 13 août. J'ai un frère et une sœur. J'ai les cheveux blonds, courts et frisés. J'ai les yeux marron. **(2)** Je m'appelle Philippe. J'ai 15 ans et mon anniversaire est le 20 juin. J'ai une sœur. J'ai les cheveux noirs, longs et ondulés. J'ai les yeux verts. **(3)** Je m'appelle André. J'ai 16 ans et mon anniversaire est le 15 janvier. J'ai deux frères. J'ai les cheveux châtains, courts et raides. J'ai les yeux bleus. **(4)** Je m'appelle Éric. J'ai 10 ans et mon anniversaire est le 8 mars. J'ai trois sœurs. J'ai les cheveux bruns, courts et en épis. J'ai les yeux marron. **(5)** Je m'appelle Mélanie. J'ai 11 ans et mon anniversaire est le 25 décembre. J'ai un frère. J'ai les cheveux roux, courts et raides. J'ai les yeux marron. **(6)** Je m'appelle Alain. J'ai 14 ans et mon anniversaire est le 19 mai. Je suis fils unique. J'ai les cheveux blonds, courts et frisés. J'ai les yeux gris.

UNIT 4 – SAYING WHERE I LIVE AND AM FROM

1. Fill in the blanks

(1) Salut. Je m'**appelle** David. J'habite dans une très grande **maison** en centre-**ville**.

(2) Bonjour. Je m'appelle Chloé. Je **suis** de Paris. Je **vis** dans un petit appartement dans la **banlieue**.

(3) Comment ça va? Je **m'**appelle Marie. Je suis **de** Calais. Je vis dans un joli **appartement** sur la côte.

(4) Salut. Je m'appelle **Pierre**. Je suis de Nouméa, en **Nouvelle-Calédonie**. J'habite dans une très **petite** maison à la montagne.

(5) **Bonjour**. Je m'appelle Daniel, j'habite à Bruxelles, en **Belgique**. Je vis dans un bâtiment **ancien** dans le centre de Bruxelles.

(6) **Salut**. Je m'appelle Béatrice. J'habite dans **une** grande maison, mais elle est un peu **moche**.

2. Multiple choice quiz: select the correct location

	a	b	c
Xavier	Brest	**Valence**	Grenoble
Samuel	**Calais**	Mende	Laval
Jean-Paul	**Limoges**	Sarlat	Lyon
Pascal	Toulouse	**Quimper**	Marmande
Céline	Brest	Biarritz	**Paris**
Aurélie	Bordeaux	Dijon	**Marseille**
Gabrièle	Saint-Tropez	Quimper	**Nice**
Patrice	Limoges	**Marmande**	Saint-Etienne
Emmanuel	Rennes	Mulhouse	**Biarritz**

1. Xavier habite à Valence.
2. Samuel habite à Calais.
3. Jean-Paul vit à Limoges.
4. Pascal habite à Quimper.
5. Céline vit à Paris.
6. Aurélie habite à Marseille.
7. Gabrièle habite à Nice.
8. Patrice vit à Marmande.
9. Emmanuel habite à Biarritz.

3. Spot the intruders: identify the words the speaker is NOT saying

Salut. Je m'appelle Julien. J'ai (~~âge~~) quatorze ans et j'habite (~~dans~~) à Dakar, (~~le~~) la capitale du Sénégal. Dans ma famille, (~~nous sommes~~) il y a quatre personnes: mes parents, (~~ma sœur~~), mon frère et moi. Mon frère (~~qui~~) s'appelle Benjamin. J'habite dans une (~~la~~) petite maison dans le centre de Dakar. Ma maison est (~~très~~) jolie.

4. Geographical mistakes: listen and correct

(1) Je m'appelle Nina. Je suis de Brest. Brest est en **Bretagne.**

(2) Je m'appelle Pierre. Je suis de Dakar. Dakar est au **Sénégal.**

(3) Je m'appelle Clémence. Je suis de Libreville. Libreville est **au Gabon.**

(4) Je m'appelle Jean. Je suis de Montréal. Montréal est au **Québec.**

(5) Je m'appelle Julie. Je suis de Casablanca. Casablanca est au **Maroc.**

(6) Je m'appelle Aurélie. Je suis de Nice. Nice est en **Provence.**

5. Spelling challenge: which city names are being spelled out?

Fill in the grid

1	NICE
2	BREST
3	LIBREVILLE
4	MONTRÉAL
5	MARMANDE
6	DAKAR
7	BAYONNE

TRANSCRIPT: Speaker spells out each word letter by letter.

 THE LANGUAGE GYM

6. Faulty translation: spot and correct the translation errors

My name is Marie. I am from **Reunion Island,** but I live in France. I am twelve. I live in Brittany, a region in the **northwest** of France. I have **red** hair and **brown** eyes. My hair is long and **straight**. I live in a small flat **on the outskirts** of Rennes with my mother, Éliane, and my two **sisters**, Sylvie and Pauline. My flat is in a **modern** building. It is ugly. My father lives in a **big** house on the **coast**. His house is **pretty** and modern.

TRANSCRIPT:

Je m'appelle Marie. Je suis de **La Réunion**, mais je vis en France. J'ai douze ans. J'habite en Bretagne, une région du **nord-ouest** de la France. J'ai les cheveux **roux** et les yeux **marron**. Mes cheveux sont longs et **raides**. Je vis dans un petit appartement **dans la banlieue** de Rennes avec ma mère, Éliane, et mes deux **sœurs**, Sylvie et Pauline. Mon appartement est dans un bâtiment **moderne**. Il est **moche**. Mon père habite dans une **grande** maison sur la **côte**. Sa maison est **jolie** et moderne.

7. Spot the missing words and write them in

(1) J'habite à Nouméa, la capitale **de** la Nouvelle-Calédonie. Nouméa est une **très** belle ville. Je vis dans un **petit** appartement dans un bâtiment moderne **en** centre-ville.

(2) J'habite avec ma famille à Cannes, une ville touristique dans le sud **de** la France. Je vis dans **une** maison moderne dans la banlieue de **la** ville.

(3) J'habite à Saint-Denis, la capitale de La Réunion. Je vis avec ma famille et **mon** chien. J'habite dans un grand appartement, **mais** il est moche et dans un bâtiment **ancien**.

(4) Je vis à Valence, **en** France. J'habite **dans** une **très** grande maison moderne sur la côte.

8. Complete the grid, as shown in the example (names are spelled out for you)

	Name	Country	Type of accommodation	House/flat location	Two details about the house/flat
1	*Anne*	*France*	*House*	*Town centre*	*1 ugly / 2 big*
2	**Caroline**	Sénégal	Flat	Coast	1 small / 2 ugly
3	**Jean**	Mali	Flat	Outskirts	1 pretty / 2 (very) small
4	**Paul**	Martinique	House	Town centre	1 big / 2 luxurious
5	**Marie**	Québec	House	Mountain	1 spacious / 2 modern
6	**Aurélie**	Gabon	House	Coast	1 big / 2 pretty
7	**Guillaume**	Belgique	Flat	Town centre	1 small / 2 modern
8	**Alexandre**	La Réunion	Flat	Oustkirts	1 pretty / 2 modern

TRANSCRIPT:

(1) Salut, je m'appelle Anne *(A N N E). Je suis française et j'habite dans une maison en centre-ville. Elle est moche, mais grande.*

(2) Salut, je m'appelle Caroline (C A R O L I N E). J'habite au Sénégal dans un appartement sur la côte. Mon appartement est petit et moche.

(3) Salut, moi c'est Jean (J E A N). Je suis du Mali et j'habite dans un appartement dans la banlieue de ma ville. Mon appartement est joli, mais très petit.

(4) Salut, moi c'est Paul (P A U L). Je suis de la Martinique. J'habite dans une maison en centre-ville. Ma maison est grande et luxueuse.

(5) Salut, moi c'est Marie (M A R I E). Je suis du Québec et je vis dans une maison à la montagne. J'aime ma maison, car elle est spacieuse et moderne.

(6) Salut, moi c'est Aurélie (A U R É L I E) et je vis au Gabon. J'habite dans une maison sur la côte. Elle est grande et jolie.

(7) Salut, je m'appelle Guillaume (G U I L L A U M E) et j'habite en Belgique, dans un appartement en centre-ville. Mon appartement est petit, mais moderne.

(8) Salut, je m'appelle Alexandre (A L E X A N D R E) et je suis de La Réunion. J'habite dans un appartement dans la banlieue. Mon appartement est joli et moderne.

9. Narrow listening: gapped translation

My name is Julien. I am **17** years old and my birthday is on **30th** August. I **live** in Biarritz, in the Basque Country, in the **southwest** of France. I live in an **old** house on the **outskirts**. I have two **sisters**, Marie and Sylvie. Marie is very **pretty** but a bit silly. Sylvie is a bit **ugly** but very **intelligent** and funny. My friend Romain **lives** in Bordeaux, but he is from Biarritz like **me**. He lives in a modern **building** in the **city centre**. He has a big dog called **Roi**. He lives in a big and **beautiful** flat.

TRANSCRIPT: Je m'appelle Julien. J'ai **17** ans et mon anniversaire est le **30** août. Je **vis** à Biarritz, dans le Pays basque, dans le **sud-ouest** de la France. J'habite dans une **vieille** maison dans la **banlieue**. J'ai deux **sœurs**, Marie et Sylvie. Marie est très **jolie,** mais un peu bête. Sylvie est un peu **moche**, mais très **intelligente** et marrante. Mon ami Romain **habite** à Bordeaux, mais il est de Biarritz comme **moi**. Il vit dans un **bâtiment** moderne en **centre-ville**. Il a un grand chien qui s'appelle **Roi**. Il habite dans un grand et **joli** appartement.

10. Listening slalom: follow the speaker from top to bottom and number the boxes accordingly

1	2	3	4	5
I live in Gabon, (1)	I am from Switzerland and (2)	I am from Belgium and (3)	I am from Morocco and (4)	I am from France and (5)
I live in Marrakesh. (4)	I live in Brussels. (3)	I live near Geneva. (2)	I live in Cannes. (5)	**near Libreville. (1)**
I am 12 and (2)	**I am 15 and (1)**	I am 14 and (5)	I am 16 and (3)	I am 13 and (4)
I live in a big house (5)	I live in a small house (2)	I live in a very small house (4)	**I live in a small flat (1)**	I live in a flat (3)
in a modern building. (1)	in an old building. (3)	in the city centre. (4)	near a lake. (2)	on the coast. (5)
I like my house (5)	**My flat is ugly (1)**	My house (2)	My flat is cosy (3)	My house is pretty (4)
and beautiful. (3)	and spacious. (4)	**but very big. (1)**	is modern. (2)	because it is big. (5)

TRANSCRIPT:

(1) Je vis au Gabon, près de Libreville. J'ai 15 ans et j'habite dans un petit appartement dans un bâtiment moderne. Mon appartement est moche, mais très grand. **(2)** Je suis de Suisse et je vis près de Genève. J'ai 12 ans et j'habite dans une petite maison près d'un lac. Ma maison est moderne. **(3)** Je suis de Belgique et je vis à Bruxelles. J'ai 16 ans et j'habite dans un appartement dans un bâtiment ancien. Mon appartement est confortable et joli. **(4)** Je suis du Maroc et je vis à Marrakesh. J'ai 13 ans et j'habite dans une très petite maison en centre-ville. Ma maison est jolie et spacieuse. **(5)** Je suis de France et je vis à Cannes. J'ai 14 ans et j'habite dans une grande maison sur la côte. J'aime ma maison car elle est grande.

11. Narrow listening: fill in the grid as shown in the example (Matéo)

	Name	Age	Birthday	Town	Accommodation	Description	Location
1	*Matéo*	*14*	*20th May*	*Marseille*	*House*	*Big*	*Coast*
2	Philippe	15	1st Jan	Cannes	Flat	Ugly	City centre
3	André	12	5th Mar	Biarritz	Flat	Pretty	Outskirts
4	Éric	11	22nd Aug	Val d'Isère	Chalet	Spacious	Mountain
5	Mélanie	18	18th Sept	Brest	House	Small	City centre
6	Pauline	31	17th Jul	Dijon	Flat	Modern	Ouskirts

TRANSCRIPT: (1) Salut, je m'appelle Matéo et j'ai 14 ans. Mon anniversaire est le 20 mai. Je suis de Marseille et j'habite dans une grande maison sur la côte. **(2)** Salut, je m'appelle Philippe et j'ai 15 ans. Mon anniversaire est le premier janvier. Je suis de Cannes et j'habite dans un appartement moche en centre-ville. **(3)** Salut, je m'appelle André et j'ai 12 ans. Mon anniversaire est le 5 mars. Je suis de Biarritz et j'habite dans un joli appartement dans la banlieue. **(4)** Salut, je m'appelle Éric et j'ai 11 ans. Mon anniversaire est le 22 août. Je suis de Val d'Isère et j'habite dans un chalet spacieux à la montagne. **(5)** Salut, je m'appelle Mélanie et j'ai 18 ans. Mon anniversaire est le 18 septembre. Je suis de Brest et j'habite dans une petite maison en centre-ville. **(6)** Salut, je m'appelle Pauline et j'ai 31 ans. Mon anniversaire est le 17 juillet. Je suis de Dijon et j'habite dans un appartement moderne dans la banlieue.

UNIT 5 – TALKING ABOUT MY FAMILY MEMBERS (AGE & RELATIONSHIPS)

1. Fill in the blanks

a. Dans ma **famille,** il y a **cinq** personnes.

b. Mon grand-père a **soixante-dix** ans.

c. Dans **ma** famille, **il y a** six **personnes**.

d. Mon **père** s'appelle **Pascal.**

e. Je m'**entends** bien avec **mon** frère **aîné.**

f. Je m'entends **mal** avec ma **mère.**

g. Je m'entends **très** bien avec mon **père.**

2. Break the flow

a. Il y a quatre personnes dans ma famille.

b. Je m'entends bien avec mes parents.

c. Mon grand-père a quatre-vingts ans.

d. Mon oncle a quarante ans.

e. Mon frère aîné s'appelle Jean.

f. Dans ma famille, il y a cinq personnes.

g. Mon père a quarante-deux ans.

3. Multiple choice quiz: select the correct age

		a	b	c
1	Julien	40	**50**	60
2	Sylvie	90	80	**70**
3	Jean	30	40	**60**
4	Pierre	60	70	**100**
5	Marina	**36**	46	56
6	Clémence	65	**85**	95
7	Éric	33	63	**73**
8	Paul	**71**	21	41
9	Émma	57	67	**47**

TRANSCRIPT:

(1) Je m'appelle **Julien** et j'ai 50 ans.
(2) Je m'appelle **Sylvie** et j'ai 70 ans.
(3) Je m'appelle **Jean** et j'ai 60 ans.
(4) Je m'appelle **Pierre** et j'ai 100 ans.
(5) Je m'appelle **Marina** et j'ai 36 ans.
(6) Je m'appelle **Clémence** et j'ai 85 ans.
(7) Je m'appelle **Éric** et j'ai 73 ans.
(8) Je m'appelle **Paul** et j'ai 71 ans.
(9) Je m'appelle **Émma** et j'ai 47 ans.

4. Spot the intruders: identify the word(s) in each sentence the speaker is NOT saying

a. Dans ma famille, il y a cinq ~~mille~~ personnes.

b. Mon oncle Pierre a quarante-~~et-un~~ ans.

c. Je m'entends ~~très~~ bien avec mes parents.

d. Mon cousin Tristan a ~~comme~~ cinquante ans.

e. Mes grands-parents ~~maternels~~ ont quatre-vingts ans.

f. Je m'entends mal avec mon cousin ~~Jean~~.

5. Listen, spot and correct the errors

a. **Ma grand-mère** a quatre-vingt-deux ans.

b. Il y a **quatre** personnes dans ma famille.

c. Dans ma famille, il y a six personnes: ma mère, mon **père** et mes trois frères.

d. Quel âge a ta sœur **aînée**?

e. Mon oncle a **soixante** ans.

f. Je m'entends **mal** avec mes parents, surtout avec **mon père.**

g. Dans ma famille, il y a **cinq** personnes.

6. Complete the words then write the number it refers to

a. (Exemple) **QUA**tre-vingt-sept (87)

b. Quatre-**VINGT**-quinze (95)

c. Vingt-**DEUX** (22)

d. **QUA**rante-trois (43)

e. **Cent** (100)

f. Quatre-vingt-**DIX**-huit (98)

g. Cin**QUANTE**-neuf (59)

h. Soixante-**QUATORZE** (74)

7. Faulty translation: spot the translation errors and correct them

ANSWERS:
a. My name is Jean-François. I am **15** years old.
b. I have blond and **short** hair.
c. I have **blue** eyes.
d. In my family there are **5** people: my father, my mother, my **sister**, my brother and me.
e. My father is **45**, my mother is **43**, my sister is **19** and my brother is **17**.
f. My uncle and my aunt are called Robert and Martine. My uncle is **60** years old and my aunt is **52**.
g. My maternal grandparents are **90** years old.
h. My paternal grandfather is **66**.

TRANSCRIPT:
a. Je m'appelle Jean-François. J'ai **15** ans.
b. J'ai les cheveux blonds et **courts**.
c. J'ai les yeux **bleus**.
d. Dans ma famille, il y a **5** personnes: mon père, ma mère, ma **sœur**, mon frère et moi.
e. Mon père a **45** ans, ma mère a **43** ans, ma sœur a **19** ans et mon frère a **17** ans.
f. Mon oncle et ma tante s'appellent Robert et Martine. Mon oncle a **60** ans et ma tante a **52** ans.
g. Mes grands-parents maternels ont **90** ans.
h. Mon grand-père paternel a **66** ans.

9. Listen, spot and correct the errors

a. Je **m'**appelle Raphaël.
b. **J'ai** quinze ans.
c. Mon anniversaire **est** le treize mai.
d. Dans ma famille, **il y a** quatre personnes: mes parents, mon frère aîné et **moi**.
e. Mon père **a** quarante ans.
f. Ma mère a quarante-**deux** ans.
g. Mon frère aîné a vingt-**et**-un ans.
h. **Je m'**entends bien avec mes parents.
i. Je m'entends mal **avec** mon frère.

8. Spot and write in the missing words

a. Je **m'**appelle Dylan.
b. Je viens **d'**Espagne.
c. J'ai **un** frère.
d. Mon anniversaire **est** le vingt mars.
e. Dans ma famille, nous **sommes** cinq personnes.
f. Il y a mon père, ma mère, mes **deux** frères et moi.
g. J'ai trente-**sept** ans. Ma mère a soixante-deux ans et mon père a soixante-**et-un** ans.
h. Mon frère **aîné** a quarante ans et mon frère **cadet** a trente-cinq ans.
i. Je m'entends **très** bien **avec** mes parents.

10. Fill in the table with the following names and add the missing ages

		Father's age	Mother's age	Sibling's age
1	Alex	56	48	18
2	Paul	43	**44**	15
3	Nina	**48**	51	**22**
4	Dylan	55	**53**	17
5	Michel	**72**	68	**39**
6	Marie	**40**	47	10

TRANSCRIPT
(1) Je m'appelle **Alex**. Mon père a 56 ans et ma mère a 48 ans. Mon frère a 18 ans.
(2) Je m'appelle **Paul**. Mon père a 43 ans et ma mère a 44 ans. Ma sœur a 15 ans.
(3) Je m'appelle **Nina**. Mon père a 48 ans et ma mère a 51 ans. Mon frère a 22 ans.
(4) Je m'appelle **Dylan**. Mon père a 55 ans et ma mère a 53 ans. Mon frère a 17 ans.
(5) Je m'appelle **Michel**. Mon père a 72 ans et ma mère a 68 ans. Mon frère a 39 ans.
(6) Je m'appelle **Marie**. Mon père a 40 ans et ma mère a 47 ans. Ma sœur a 10 ans.

11. Translate the ten sentences you hear into English

a. **Je m'appelle Sylvie** = My name is Sylvie
b. **J'ai quinze ans** = I am 15
c. **Dans ma famille, il y a cinq personnes** = In my family, there are 5 people
d. **Mon père, ma mère et mes deux frères** = My father, my mother and my two brothers
e. **Mon père a 46 ans** = My father is 46
f. **Ma mère a 39 ans** = My mother is 39
g. **Mes sœurs ont 17 et 21 ans** = My sisters are 17 and 21
h. **Mon grand-père a 76 ans** = My grandfather is 76
i. **Ma grand-mère a 69 ans** = My grandmother is 69
j. **J'ai une tortue qui a 3 ans** = I have a 3-year-old turtle

12. Narrow listening: gapped translation

My name is Paul. I am from **Biarritz**. I am **13** years old. My birthday is on **30th January**. I have **blond**, long and **straight** hair. I have **blue** eyes. In my family there are **5** people: my **stepfather**, my mother and my two sisters. My older sister is **16** years old. My younger sister is **11** years old. I **get along** with my parents. My **maternal** grandfather lives with us. He is **85** years old. I get along with him.

TRANSCRIPT: Je m'appelle Paul. Je suis de **Biarritz**. J'ai **13** ans. Mon anniversaire est le **30 janvier**. J'ai les cheveux **blonds**, longs et **raides**. J'ai les yeux **bleus**. Dans ma famille, il y a **5** personnes: mon **beau-père**, ma mère et mes deux sœurs. Ma sœur aînée a **16** ans. Ma sœur cadette a **11** ans. Je **m'entends bien** avec mes parents. Mon grand-père **maternel** habite avec nous. Il a **85** ans. Je m'entends bien avec lui.

13. Listening slalom: follow the speaker from top to bottom and number the boxes accordingly

1	2	3	4	5
Name: Hélène (1)	Name: Philippe (2)	Name: Marie (3)	Name: Xavier (4)	Name: Jean (5)
I am 17 (4)	**I am 16 (1)**	I am 20 (5)	I am 11 (2)	I am 30 (3)
Birthday: 25 Oct (2)	Birthday: 20 June (3)	**Birthday: 31 Dec (1)**	Birthday: 15 Mar (4)	Birthday: 7 Jan (5)
My mother is 50 (5)	**My mother is 48 (1)**	My mother is 44 (4)	My mother is 39 (2)	My mother is 62 (3)
My father is 49 (4)	My father is 43 (2)	My father is 53 (5)	My father is 64 (3)	**My father is 52 (1)**
My grandad is 81 (5)	My grandad is 75 (3)	**My grandad is 76 (1)**	My grandad is 73 (2)	My grandad is 90 (4)
My grandma is 68 (1)	My grandma is 80 (4)	My grandma is 81 (2)	My grandma is 72 (3)	My grandma is 79 (5)

TRANSCRIPT:

(1) Salut, je m'appelle **Hélène** et j'ai 16 ans. Mon anniversaire est le 31 décembre. Ma mère a 48 ans et mon père a 52 ans. Mon grand-père a 76 ans et ma grand-mère a 68 ans. **(2)** Salut, je m'appelle **Philippe** et j'ai 11 ans. Mon anniversaire est le 25 octobre. Ma mère a 39 ans et mon père a 43 ans. Mon grand-père a 73 ans et ma grand-mère a 81ans. **(3)** Salut, je m'appelle **Marie** et j'ai 30 ans. Mon anniversaire est le 20 juin. Ma mère a 62 ans et mon père a 64 ans. Mon grand-père a 75 ans et ma grand-mère a 72 ans. **(4)** Salut, je m'appelle **Xavier** et j'ai 17 ans. Mon anniversaire est le 15 mars. Ma mère a 44 ans et mon père a 49 ans. Mon grand-père a 90 ans et ma grand-mère a 80 ans. **(5)** Salut, je m'appelle **Jean** et j'ai 20 ans. Mon anniversaire est le 7 janvier. Ma mère a 50 ans et mon père a 53 ans. Mon grand-père a 81 ans et ma grand-mère a 79 ans.

14. Narrow listening: listen and fill in the missing details on the grid

	Name	Age	Birthday	Family size	Older sibling's age	Mother's age	Father's age
1	**Andréa**	**12**	20 June	**5**	16	**39**	41
2	**Philippe**	14	**14 Dec**	5	**18**	**42**	44
3	**Sophie**	**11**	15 Sep	4	**21**	43	**46**
4	**Éric**	13	**9 Aug**	5	**15**	39	**40**
5	**Myriam**	28	**31 Jul**	**6**	31	**56**	55

TRANSCRIPT:

(1) Je m'appelle **Andréa** et j'ai 12 ans. Mon anniversaire est le 20 juin. Il y a 5 personnes dans ma famille. Mon frère cadet a 5 ans et ma sœur aînée a 16 ans. Ma mère a 39 ans et mon père a 41 ans.

(2) Je m'appelle **Philippe** et j'ai 14 ans. Mon anniversaire est le 14 décembre. Il y a 5 personnes dans ma famille. Ma sœur cadette a 8 ans et mon frère aîné a 18 ans. Ma mère a 42 ans et mon père a 44 ans.

(3) Je m'appelle **Sophie** et j'ai 11 ans. Mon anniversaire est le 15 septembre. Il y a 4 personnes dans ma famille. J'ai seulement un frère aîné et il a 21 ans. Ma mère a 43 ans et mon père a 46 ans.

(4) Je m'appelle **Éric** et j'ai 13 ans. Mon anniversaire est le 9 août. Il y a 5 personnes dans ma famille. Mon frère cadet a 9 ans et mon frère aîné a 15 ans. Ma mère a 39 ans et mon père a 40 ans.

(5) Je m'appelle **Myriam** et j'ai 28 ans. Mon anniversaire est le 31 juillet. Il y a 6 personnes dans ma famille. Mes deux sœurs cadettes ont 10 et 11 ans et ma sœur aînée a 31 ans. Ma mère a 56 ans et mon père a 55 ans.

UNIT 6 – DESCRIBING MYSELF AND ANOTHER FAMILY MEMBER

1. Multiple choice quiz: select the correct adjective for each sentence

		a	b	c
1	My father is…	**generous**	fun	muscular
2	My mother is…	fat	**intelligent**	thin
3	My older sister is…	stupid	**tall**	muscular
4	My younger sister is…	tall	short	**pretty**
5	My brother is…	**friendly**	unfriendly	ugly
6	My cousin Paul is…	big	**strong**	small
7	My cousin Marie is…	lazy	bad	**boring**
8	My grandfather is…	**mean**	stubborn	annoying
9	My grandmother is...	generous	nice	**fun**
10	My girlfriend is…	patient	fat	**muscular**

TRANSCRIPT: (1) Mon père est généreux. (2) Ma mère est intelligente. (3) Ma sœur aînée est grande. (4) Ma sœur cadette est belle. (5) Mon frère est sympa. (6) Mon cousin Paul est fort. (7) Ma cousine Marie est ennuyeuse. (8) Mon grand-père est méchant. (9) Ma grand-mère est amusante. (10) Ma petite amie est musclée.

2. Split sentences: listen and match

1. Didier	3. Fun
2. Sylvie	9. Boring
3. Morgan	4. Short
4. Kevin	2. Tall
5. Marine	10. Good-looking
6. Ariane	**1. Mean**
7. Éric	5. Muscular
8. Paul	6. Ugly
9. Adeline	8. Stubborn
10. Manu	7. Strong

TRANSCRIPT: (1) Mon cousin Didier est très méchant. (2) Mon amie Sylvie est grande. (3) Morgan est amusant. (4) Mon frère Kevin est petit. (5) Mon amie Marine est musclée. (6) Ma cousine Ariane est moche. (7) Mon ami Éric est fort. (8) Mon ami Paul est têtu. (9) Ma sœur Adeline est ennuyeuse. (10) Mon ami Manu est beau.

3. Spot the intruders: identify the word in each sentence the speaker is NOT saying

a. Mon frère est ~~très~~ beau.

b. Mon oncle ~~Paul~~ a quarante ans. Il est assez marrant.

c. Je m'entends très bien avec mon père parce qu'il est ~~assez~~ généreux.

d. Mon cousin Yann n'est pas ~~très~~ grand.

e. Ma sœur est de ~~la~~ taille moyenne.

f. Ma petite amie est ~~trop~~ bavarde.

4. Spot the differences and correct your text

a. Ma **mère** est très patiente.
b. Ma mère est très **travailleuse**.
c. Dans ma famille, il y a cinq personnes: ma mère, mon **beau**-père, mes deux frères et moi.
d. Comment **ça va**?
e. Mon oncle a soixante-**dix** ans, mais il est très **fort**.
f. Je m'entends mal avec mes parents, surtout avec ma mère car elle est très **stricte**.
g. Dans ma famille, nous sommes tous **grands**.

5. Categories: listen to the words below and classify them in positive and negative

ADJECTIFS POSITIFS	ADJECTIFS NÉGATIFS
Intelligent	Stupide
Beau	Moche
Sympa	Antipathique
Marrant	Méchant
Amusant	Ennuyeux
Patient	Impatient
Généreux	Égoïste
Travailleur	Paresseux

TRANSCRIPT:
(1) Intelligent (2) Beau
(3) Stupide (4) Sympa
(5) Moche
(6) Antipathique
(7) Marrant (8) Méchant
(9) Ennuyeux (10)
Amusant (11) Patient (12)
Généreux (13) Impatient
(14) Égoïste (15)
Paresseux (16) Travailleur

 THE LANGUAGE GYM

6. Faulty translation: spot and correct the translation errors

a. My name is Jean-Paul. I am **14** years old. I have **blond** hair and green eyes. I am **short**, muscular and **very** handsome. I am friendly, talkative and quite **funny**.

b. My mother is called Patricia. She is **40** years old. She is **tall**, slim and very **pretty**. She is generous, but a bit **strict**.

c. My father is called Robert. He is **63** years old. He is neither tall nor short. He is quite **ugly**. He is very generous, **friendly** and patient.

d. My sister is called Carla. She is **16**. She is quite tall and **fat**. She is unfriendly and **stubborn**. She is also quite **impatient** and lazy.

TRANSCRIPT: (a) Je m'appelle Jean-Paul. J'ai 14 ans. J'ai les cheveux blonds et les yeux verts. Je suis petit, musclé et très beau. Je suis sympa, bavard et assez marrant. **(b)** Ma mère s'appelle Patricia. Elle a 40 ans. Elle est grande, mince et très belle. Elle est généreuse, mais un peu stricte. **(c)** Mon père s'appelle Robert. Il a 63 ans. Il est ni grand, ni petit. Il est assez moche. Il est très généreux, sympa et patient. **(d)** Ma sœur s'appelle Carla. Elle a 16 ans. Elle est assez grande et grosse. Elle est antipathique et têtue. Elle est aussi assez impatiente et paresseuse.

7. Spot the missing words and write them in

a. Je m'appelle David et **(je suis)** très travailleur.

b. Mon frère est **(trop)** paresseux.

c. Ma mère est têtue **(et)** antipathique.

d. Mon frère est de **(taille)** moyenne.

e. Mes parents **(sont)** très timides.

f. Ma sœur **(aînée)** est très généreuse.

g. Je déteste **(mon)** cousin, car il est **(très)** têtu.

8. Listen and complete with the correct masculine or feminine ending

a. Elle est très **grandE**
b. Ils sont très **MéchantS**
c. Ma mère et mon père sont très **paresseuX**
d. Je suis **petitE** et **patientE**
e. Tu es si **amusanT**!
f. Elles sont **méchantES**!
g. Leurs **fiLLES** sont très **grosSES**
h. Mes **fiLS** sont très **travailleurS**
i. Tu es si **marrantE**!

9. Listen and fill in the grid

	Person	Description
1	My father is	tall and friendly
2	My mother is	short and talkative
3	My sister is	blond and stubborn
4	My brother is	short and lazy
5	My cousin Paul is	tall and slim
6	My cousin Marie is	neither tall nor short
7	My grandfather is	generous and nice/likeable
8	My grandmother is	strict and annoying
9	My best friend is	friendly and funny

TRANSCRIPT:
(1) Mon père est grand et sympa.
(2) Ma mère est petite et bavarde.
(3) Ma sœur est blonde et têtue.
(4) Mon frère est petit et paresseux.
(5) Mon cousin Paul est grand et mince.
(6) Ma cousine Marie n'est ni grande ni petite.
(7) Mon grand-père est généreux et aimable.
(8) Ma grand-mère est stricte et pénible.
(9) Ma meilleure amie est sympa et marrante.

10. Translate the ten sentences you hear into English

1. My name is Romain.
Je m'appelle Romain.
2. I am 14.
J'ai quatorze ans.
3. I am a redhead and have green eyes.
J'ai les cheveux roux et les yeux verts.
4. There are 3 persons in my family.
Il y a trois personnes dans ma famille.
5. My father is 46 years old.
Mon père a 46 ans.
6. My mother is 39 years old.
Ma mère a 39 ans.
7. My brother is 16 years old.
Mon frère a 16 ans.

8. My father is tall, strong and fun.
Mon père est grand, fort et marrant.
9. My mother is short, slim and very strict.
Ma mère est petite, mince et très stricte.
10. My brother and I are very tall, fat and talkative.
Mon frère et moi sommes très grands, gros et bavards.

11. Narrow listening: gapped translation

My name is Paul. I love my parents. They are a bit **strict**, but very generous, **likeable** and hard-working. I have **two** brothers and one sister. My older brother is very annoying: he is **noisy**, lazy, **unfriendly**, **mean** and too talkative. My younger brother is charming: he is nice, **generous**, patient, **helpful** and hard-working. My sister is very pretty and **intelligent**, but very boring. I also have a **girlfriend**. Her name is Pauline. She is tall, **interesting**, pretty and she is also very **funny**.

TRANSCRIPT: Je m'appelle Paul. J'adore mes parents. Ils sont un peu **stricts**, mais très généreux, **aimables** et travailleurs. J'ai **deux** frères et une sœur. Mon frère aîné est très pénible: il est **bruyant**, paresseux, **antipathique, méchant,** et trop bavard. Mon frère cadet est charmant: il est sympa, **généreux,** patient, **serviable** et travailleur. Ma sœur est très jolie et **intelligente,** mais très ennuyeuse. J'ai aussi une **petite amie**. Son nom est Pauline. Elle est grande, **intéressante,** belle et elle est aussi très **marrante.**

---

12. Listening slalom: follow the speaker from top to bottom and number the boxes accordingly

1	2	3	4	5
My name is Naomi (1)	My name is Anne (2)	My name is Manuela (3)	My name is Kevin (4)	My name is Jean-Charles (5)
I am 15 years old (3)	**I am 17 years old (1)**	I am 18 years old (4)	I am 13 years old (5)	I am 12 years old (2)
I am tall and fat (4)	I am neither tall nor short (3)	**I am tall and slim (1)**	I am not very tall (2)	I am short and slim (5)
My older brother is short and slim (4)	My older sister is short and slim (2)	My younger brother is short and slim (3)	My older sister is short and very pretty (5)	**My younger brother is tall and strong (1)**
I like her (5)	I get along very well with him (3)	I like her a lot (2)	**I get along with him (1)**	I don't get along with him (4)
because he is likeable and positive (3)	because she is generous (5)	because he is mean (4)	because she is fun (2)	**because he is patient and helpful. (1)**
and likeable. (2)	Furthermore, he is very funny. (3)	**He is also very generous and kind. (1)**	and funny (5)	And stubborn. (4)

TRANSCRIPT: (1) Je m'appelle Naomi. J'ai 17 ans et je suis grande et mince. Mon petit frère est grand et fort. Je m'entends bien avec lui parce qu'il est patient et serviable. Il est aussi très généreux et sympa. **(2)** Je m'appelle Anne et j'ai 12 ans. Je ne suis pas très grande. Ma sœur aînée est petite et mince. Je l'aime beaucoup, car elle est marrante et aimable. **(3)** Je m'appelle Manuela et j'ai 15 ans. Je ne suis ni grande, ni petite. Mon frère cadet est petit et mince. Je m'entends bien avec lui car il est aimable et positif. En plus, il est très marrant. **(4)** Je m'appelle Kevin et j'ai 18 ans. Je suis grand et gros. Mon frère aîné est petit et mince. Je ne m'entends pas bien avec lui car il est méchant et têtu. **(5)** Je m'appelle Jean-Charles et j'ai 13 ans. Je suis petit et mince. Ma sœur aînée est petite et très belle. Je l'aime parce qu'elle est généreuse et marrante.

---

13. Narrow listening: fill in the grid

	Name	Name of older sibling	Age of older sibling	Birthday of older sibling	Character of older sibling	Appearance of older sibling
1	**Philippe**	Jules	18	20th June	Lazy	Ugly
2	**Andréa**	Lucie	17	30th Dec	Boring	Pretty
3	**Éric**	Marta	19	22nd April	Mean	Fat
4	**Mélanie**	Caroline	21	1st Jan	Funny	Tall

TRANSCRIPT: (1) Je m'appelle Philippe. Mon frère aîné s'appelle Jules et il a 18 ans. Son anniversaire est le 20 juin. Il est paresseux et moche! **(2)** Je m'appelle Andréa. Ma sœur aînée s'appelle Lucie et elle a 17 ans. Son anniversaire est le 30 décembre. Elle est ennuyeuse, mais jolie. **(3)** Je m'appelle Éric. Ma sœur aînée s'appelle Marta et elle a 19 ans. Son anniversaire est le 22 avril. Elle est méchante et grosse. **(4)** Je m'appelle Mélanie. Ma sœur aînée s'appelle Caroline et elle a 21 ans. Son anniversaire est le premier janvier. Elle est marrante et grande.

 **THE LANGUAGE GYM**

UNIT 7 – TALKING ABOUT PETS

1. Multiple choice quiz

		a	b	c
1	At home we have…	**4 pets**	2 pets	5 pets
2	I have a…	turtle	**dog**	cat
3	My brother has a…	turtle	**fish**	parrot
4	My older sister has a…	lizard	**rabbit**	duck
5	My younger sister has a…	**mouse**	fish	horse
6	My mother has a…	**cat**	dog	parrot
7	My father has a…	bird	**horse**	dog
8	My grandparents have two…	**dogs**	horses	rabbits
9	My best friend has a…	lizard	dog	**snake**
10	My girlfriend has a…	fish	cat	**dog**

TRANSCRIPT:

1. À la maison nous avons 4 animaux.
2. J'ai un chien.
3. Mon frère a un poisson.
4. Ma sœur aînée a un lapin.
5. Ma sœur cadette a une souris.
6. Ma mère a un chat.
7. Mon père a un cheval.
8. Mes grands-parents ont deux chiens.
9. Ma meilleure amie a un serpent.
10. Ma petite amie a un chien.

2. Split sentences: listen and match

1. Alexandra	a. A dog
2. Sylvie	b. A rabbit
3. Carmen	c. A parrot
4. Jean	**d. A fish**
5. Fabrice	e. A cat
6. Pascal	f. A horse
7. Jules	g. Two dogs
8. Véronique	h. Two turtles
9. Robert	i. Two mice
10. Simone	j. A mouse

ANSWERS: 1d 2a 3b 4c 5g 6e 7i 8f 9j 10h

TRANSCRIPT: **(1)** Je m'appelle Alexandra et j'ai un poisson. **(2)** Je m'appelle Sylvie et j'ai un chien **(3)** Je m'appelle Carmen et j'ai un lapin. **(4)** Je m'appelle Jean et j'ai un perroquet. **(5)** Je m'appelle Fabrice et j'ai deux chiens. **(6)** Je m'appelle Pascal et j'ai un chat. **(7)** Je m'appelle Jules et j'ai deux souris. **(8)** Je m'appelle Véronique et j'ai un cheval. **(9)** Je m'appelle Robert et j'ai une souris. **(10)** Je m'appelle Simone et j'ai deux tortues.

4. Spot the differences and correct your text

a. Mon chien est très **beau**.
b. Mon chat est très **ennuyeux**.
c. Nous avons quatre animaux: un chien, un **oiseau,** un perroquet et un **cochon d'Inde**.
d. Tu as un **animal**?
e. Mon oncle a **un chien** et **une araignée** chez lui.
f. Ma sœur a un **rat** très **marrant**.
g. Nous avons deux **lapins** et un **canard** chez nous.
h. Paul a un très grand **chat** noir chez lui!

3. Spot the intruders: identify the word in each sentence the speaker is NOT saying

a. Mon frère a un ~~grand~~ chien.
b. Ma meilleure amie ~~n'~~a ~~pas~~ deux animaux.
c. Mes grands-parents ont deux ~~petits~~ chevaux.
d. La tortue ~~verte~~ de mon frère s'appelle Kura.
e. Ma petite amie a un chat ~~blanc~~.
f. Mon chien ~~marron~~ est mignon, mais un peu paresseux.
g. J'ai deux poissons ~~orange~~.

5. Categories: listen to the sentences and write in any adjectives or nouns you hear into the table

	NOMS (nouns)	ADJECTIFS (adjectives)
1	chat	petit
2	chien	grand
3	tortue	verte
4	poisson	ennuyeux
5	canard	bruyant
6	lapin	moche
7	araignée	marrante
8	cheval	blanc

TRANSCRIPT:

1. J'ai un petit chat.
2. J'ai un grand chien.
3. Nous avons une tortue verte.
4. J'ai un poisson ennuyeux.
5. J'ai un canard bruyant.
6. J'ai un lapin moche.
7. J'ai une araignée marrante.
8. J'ai un cheval blanc.

 **THE LANGUAGE GYM**

18

6. Spot the missing words and write them in

Je m'appelle Jean. J'ai **(trois)** animaux: un chien **(qui)** s'appelle Rufus, un chat qui **(s')** appelle Tarzan et **(un)** serpent qui s'appelle Boa. Rufus **(a)** trois ans. Il est noir et blanc. Il est **(très)** gros et tranquille. Tarzan est tigré et **(un peu)** distant. Il a **(de)** grands yeux verts. Il est intelligent, mais **(très)** ennuyeux. Il a quatre ans. Boa est un très grand serpent **(vert)**. Il a un an.

7. Fill in the blanks

Chez moi, nous avons trois **animaux**: un chien, un **chat** et un **rat**. Mon chien s'**appelle** Bandit. Il est **noir**. Je l'aime parce qu'il est **mignon** et **marrant**. Mon lapin s'appelle Zorro. Il est **blanc** et **marron**. Il est très **gros** et **amusant**. Mon rat s'appelle Rico. Il est **petit** et blanc. Il est très intelligent et **rapide**. Je l'**adore**.

8. Faulty translation: correct the translation

My name is Robert. I am **sixteen** years old and I live in Marseille. In my family, there are **four** people: my parents, my **younger** brother, Jean and myself. Jean is **ten** years old and is very **funny**. We have three pets: a parrot who is called Léo, a **dog** who is called Bingo and a **guinea pig** who is called Casper. Léo is very talkative. Bingo is **fat** and Casper is **funny**, like my brother.

TRANSCRIPT: Je m'appelle Robert. J'ai **16** ans et j'habite à Marseille. Dans ma famille, il y a **4** personnes: mes parents, mon frère **cadet**, Jean, et moi. Jean a **10** ans et il est très **marrant**. Nous avons trois animaux: un perroquet qui s'appelle Léo, un **chien** qui s'appelle Bingo et un **cochon d'Inde** qui s'appelle Casper. Léo est très bavard. Bingo est **gros** et Casper est **marrant**, comme mon frère.

9. Listen and fill in the grid

	Family member	Description
1	My father is	funny
2	My mother is	hard-working
3	My sister is	intelligent
4	My brother is	talkative
5	My cousin Paul is	helpful
6	My cousin Marie is	boring
7	My grandfather is	generous
8	My grandmother is	nice/friendly

TRANSCRIPT:
1. Mon père est marrant.
2. Ma mère est travailleuse.
3. Ma sœur est intelligente.
4. Mon frère est bavard.
5. Mon cousin Paul est serviable.
6. Ma cousine Marie est ennuyeuse.
7. Mon grand-père est généreux.
8. Ma grand-mère est sympa.

10. Translate the ten sentences you hear into English

1. In my family there are five people.
2. My two younger sisters are called Adeline and Marine.
3. My parents are very likeable and patient.
4. Marine is very generous and helpful.
5. Adeline is very lazy and boring.
6. We have six pets.
7. We have two dogs, Rex and Reine. They are very pretty.
8. I have a cat, Félix. He is very fat and lazy.
9. I have a rat, Rio. He is very funny and quick.
10. I like my family a lot.

TRANSCRIPT:
1. Dans ma famille il y a cinq personnes.
2. Mes deux sœurs cadettes s'appellent Adeline et Marine.
3. Mes parents sont très aimables et patients.
4. Marine est très généreuse et serviable.
5. Adeline est très paresseuse et ennuyeuse.
6. Nous avons six animaux.
7. Nous avons deux chiens, Rex et Reine. Ils sont très beaux.
8. J'ai un chat, Félix. Il est très gros et paresseux.
9. J'ai un rat, Rio. Il est très marrant et rapide.
10. J'aime beaucoup ma famille.

11. Sentence puzzle: rewrite correctly

a. J'ai un rat gris, un lapin très blanc et un chat marron.

b. Mon chat s'appelle Grassouillet parce qu'il mange beaucoup.

c. Mon ami Paul a un très grand serpent, noir et vert qui s'appelle Venin.

d. Nous avons une tortue verte qui s'appelle Caroline et une souris marron qui s'appelle Mascotte.

12. Narrow listening: gapped translation

My name is Patricia. I am **thirteen** years old, and **I live** in London. In my family there are **five** people: my **stepfather**, my mother, my **older** brother, my **stepsister** and me. We have a few **pets**. Firstly, we have a **huge** dog called Maximus. He is **black** and beautiful. He is very **strong** and eats **a lot**. We also have a **turtle** called Leonardo. My turtle is small, green and **funny**. She is very quiet. Finally, we have a **parrot** called Charlie. He is very **talkative** and cute. He is red, **blue** and **yellow**. I love my pets.

TRANSCRIPT:

Je m'appelle Patricia. J'ai **treize** ans, et **j'habite** à Londres. Dans ma famille il y a **cinq** personnes: mon **beau-père**, ma mère, mon frère **aîné**, ma **demi-sœur** et moi. Nous avons quelques **animaux**. Premièrement, nous avons un chien **énorme** qui s'appelle Maximus. Il est **noir** et beau. Il est très **fort** et il mange **beaucoup**. Nous avons aussi une **tortue** qui s'appelle Leonardo. Ma tortue est petite, verte et **marrante**. Elle est très tranquille. Finalement, nous avons un **perroquet** qui s'appelle Charlie. Il est très **bavard** et mignon. Il est rouge, **bleu** et **jaune**. J'adore mes animaux.

---

13. Listening slalom: follow the speaker from top to bottom and number the boxes accordingly

1	2	3	4	5
We have 3 (1)	I have (2)	My friend has (3)	My grandparents have (4)	My friend has (5)
four pets at home. (2)	**pets at home. (1)**	five pets at home. (3)	six pets at home. (4)	one pet at home: (5)
A blue fish, (2)	Two big black dogs, (3)	**A green turtle, (1)**	a big fat cat. (5)	Three fat, white guinea pigs, (4)
He is black and white. (5)	a big brown dog (4)	a beautiful yellow bird, (2)	**very slow and funny, (1)**	a yellow parrot (3)
which is talkative and funny (3)	**a cute and fat dog, (1)**	a very fat duck (4)	a cute guinea pig and (2)	He is very lazy (5)
and boring. (5)	and a very cute black rabbit. (4)	**and a goldfish. (1)**	a fun white mouse. (2)	and two pretty Siamese cats. (3)

TRANSCRIPT:

(1) Nous avons trois animaux à la maison. Une tortue verte, très lente et marrante, un chien mignon et gros, et un poisson rouge.
(2) J'ai quatre animaux à la maison. Un poisson bleu, un joli oiseau jaune, un cochon d'Inde mignon et une souris blanche marrante.
(3) Mon ami à cinq animaux chez lui. Deux grands chiens noirs, un perroquet jaune qui est bavard et marrant, et deux jolis chats siamois.
(4) Mes grands-parents ont six animaux chez eux. Trois gros cochons d'Inde blancs, un grand chien marron, un très gros canard, et un lapin noir très mignon.
(5) Mon amie a un animal chez elle: un grand et gros chat. Il est noir et blanc. Il est très paresseux et ennuyeux.

---

14. Narrow listening: fill in the grid

	Name	Age	Appearance	Character	Type of pet	Pet description (3 details)
1	**Jean-Michel**	13	Strong	Funny	Parrot	Red and yellow / (very) talkative
2	**Mariane**	15	Pretty	Talkative	Duck	Black and brown / (quite) cute
3	**Pierre**	11	Short	Nice	Fish	Green and blue / Fat
4	**Hélène**	18	Tall	Hard-working	Guinea pig	White and Brown / Fat

TRANSCRIPT:

(1) Je m'appelle Jean-Michel et j'ai 13 ans. Je suis fort et marrant. Chez moi j'ai un perroquet. Il est rouge et jaune et très bavard. **(2)** Je m'appelle Mariane et j'ai 15 ans. Je suis belle et bavarde. J'ai un canard. Il est noir et marron et assez mignon. **(3)** Je m'appelle Pierre et j'ai 11 ans. Je suis petit et sympa. J'ai un poisson vert et bleu. Il est gros! **(4)** Je m'appelle Hélène et j'ai 18 ans. Je suis grande et travailleuse. Chez moi, j'ai un cochon d'Inde blanc et marron. Il est gros.

UNIT 8 – TALKING ABOUT JOBS

1. Multiple choice quiz: select the correct job

	a	b	c
Élise	accountant	**nurse**	housewife
Rose	lawyer	farmer	**mechanic**
Pascal	engineer	businessman	**doctor**
Paul	househusband	**singer**	cook
Anne	**waitress**	receptionist	housewife
Alice	**farmer**	actress	doctor
Martine	teacher	**astronaut**	postman
Samuel	lawyer	**worker**	mechanic
Léon	policeman	singer	**cook**
Léa	**student**	doctor	farmer

TRANSCRIPT: (1) Je m'appelle Élise et je suis infirmière. **(2)** Je m'appelle Rose et je suis mécanicienne. **(3)** Je m'appelle Pascal et je suis médecin. **(4)** Je m'appelle Paul et je suis chanteur. **(5)** Je m'appelle Anne et je suis serveuse. **(6)** Je m'appelle Alice et je suis fermière. **(7)** Je m'appelle Martine et je suis astronaute. **(8)** Je m'appelle Samuel et je suis ouvrier. **(9)** Je m'appelle Léon et je suis cuisinier. **(10)** Je m'appelle Léa et je suis étudiante.

3. Split sentences: listen and match

1. Yvan		a. worker
2. Sylvie		b. lawyer
3. Paul		c. doctor
4. Philippe		d. cook
5. Caroline		e. accountant
6. Jean		f. hairdresser
7. Véronique		g. teacher
8. Jules		h. mechanic
9. Robert		i. footballer
10. Marie		**j. actor**

TRANSCRIPT: (1) Je m'appelle Yvan et je suis acteur. **(2)** Je m'appelle Sylvie et je suis ouvrière. **(3)** Je m'appelle Paul et je suis avocat. **(4)** Je m'appelle Philippe et je suis cuisinier. **(5)** Je m'appelle Caroline et je suis médecin. **(6)** Je m'appelle Jean et je suis comptable. **(7)** Je m'appelle Véronique et je suis coiffeuse. **(8)** Je m'appelle Jules et je suis mécanicien. **(9)** Je m'appelle Robert et je suis footballeur. **(10)** Je m'appelle Marie et je suis professeure. (1j, 2a, 3b, 4d, 5c, 6e, 7f, 8h, 9i, 10g)

5. Listen, spot and correct the errors

Je m'appelle **Marie**. Je suis de Biarritz. Ma personne préférée dans ma famille, c'est ma **grand-mère**. Elle est timide, mais très **aimable**. Ma **grand-mère** est comptable, mais maintenant elle ne travaille pas. Je déteste mon **oncle**. Il est intelligent, mais très antipathique. Mon **oncle** est **professeur,** mais il déteste son travail car c'est **stressant** et ennuyeux. Il travaille dans un **collège** à Biarritz. Chez moi, j'ai une **tortue** qui s'appelle Donatello. Elle est lente mais très **amusante**, comme ma sœur Cassandra.

2. Listening for detail: did you hear the masculine or the feminine form?

MASCULINE	FEMININE
acteur	**actrice**
cuisinier	**cuisinière**
homme d'affaires	femme d'affaires
fermier	**fermière**
travailleur	**travailleuse**
avocat	**avocate**
ennuyeux	ennuyeuse
actif	**active**
marrant	marrante

4. Spot the intruders

Je m'appelle **Jean**-Marc et je vais parler de ma famille. Dans ma famille, nous sommes trois **personnes**: mon père, ma mère, **mon frère** et moi. Mon père s'appelle Pascal. Il a cinquante-**six** ans. Il est **très** grand et un peu gros. Il est chauve. Il est sympathique et **aussi** travailleur. Il travaille comme **un** comptable. Il **n'**aime **pas** cela, car c'est un travail bien payé. Ma mère travaille comme **une** coiffeuse. Elle adore ça **travail** car **lui** c'est très amusant et gratifiant. Moi, je voudrais travailler comme **un** cuisinier et être connu comme Gordon Ramsay.

6. Categories: listen to the sentences and classify the words

	NOMS (nouns)	ADJECTIFS (adjectives)
1	**Réceptionniste**	**Facile**
2	**Musicien**	**Amusant**
3	**Professeur**	**Gratifiant**
4	**Avocate**	**Stimulant**
5	**Femme d'affaires**	**Intéressant**
6	**Fermier**	**Actif**

TRANSCRIPT:
(1) Je suis réceptionniste, c'est facile. **(2)** Je suis musicien, c'est amusant. **(3)** Je suis professeur, c'est gratifiant. **(4)** Je suis avocate, c'est stimulant. **(5)** Je suis femme d'affaires, c'est intéressant. **(6)** Je suis fermier, c'est actif.

7. Spot the missing words and write them in

Je m'appelle Marie. Dans ma famille **(il y a)** quatre personnes. Mon père s'appelle Émilien et **(il est)** avocat.

(Il) aime son travail, car c'est **(très)** stimulant. Cependant, **(parfois)** c'est stressant. Ma mère est femme **(au)**

foyer et elle aime assez **(son)** travail. Elle dit **(que)** c'est très gratifiant. Chez moi, j'ai un chien **(qui)** s'appelle

Calin. Il est très **(grand et)** amusant! Il n'aime pas les chats.

8. Faulty translation: correct the errors

My name is Philippe. I am **eighteen** years old and live in Casablanca, in Morocco. In my family, there are **five** persons. I have a very funny **guinea pig** called Jeannot. My father works as a **director** in a **company** in the town centre. He does not like his job because it is **difficult**. My mother is a doctor. She likes her job a lot because it is **stimulating** and **exciting**.

TRANSCRIPT:

Je m'appelle Philippe. J'ai **18** ans et je vis à Casablanca, au Maroc. Dans ma famille, il y a **5** personnes. J'ai un **cochon d'Inde** très amusant qui s'appelle Jeannot. Mon père travaille comme **directeur** dans une **entreprise** en centre-ville. Il n'aime pas son travail car c'est **difficile**. Ma mère est médecin. Elle aime beaucoup son travail car c'est **stimulant** et **passionnant**.

9. Listen and fill in the grid

	Person	Job
1	My father	Cook
2	My mother	Lawyer
3	My older brother	Gardener
4	My younger brother	Waiter
5	My sister	Businesswoman
6	My best friend	Singer
7	My girlfriend	Doctor
8	My grandfather	Accountant

TRANSCRIPT:

1. Mon père est cuisinier.

2. Ma mère est avocate.

3. Mon frère aîné est jardinier.

4. Mon frère cadet est serveur.

5. Ma sœur est femme d'affaires.

6. Ma meilleure amie est chanteuse.

7. Ma petite amie est médecin.

8. Mon grand-père est comptable.

10. Translate the sentences into English
1. In my family, there are 3 people: my parents and me.
2. My parents are very likeable, but strict.
3. My father is a worker.
4. He does not like his job, because it is tiring.
5. My mother is a waitress in a restaurant.
6. She likes her job because it is fun.
7. I do not work.
8. I am a student at the university.
9. I love it because it is stimulating.

TRANSCRIPT:
1. Dans ma famille, il y a trois personnes: mes parents et moi.
2. Mes parents sont très aimables, mais stricts.
3. Mon père est ouvrier.
4. Il n'aime pas son travail, car c'est fatigant.
5. Ma mère est serveuse dans un restaurant.
6. Elle aime son travail car c'est amusant.
7. Je ne travaille pas.
8. Je suis étudiant à l'université.
9. J'adore ça, car c'est stimulant.

11. Listen, spot and correct the errors

a. Je travaill**E** à la campagne.

b. Ma mère travaill**E** comme cuisinière.

c. Mon père **EST** coiffeur.

d. Mes frères ne travaillent p**AS**.

e. Ma petite amie est act**RICE**.

f. Mon meilleur ami est pomp**IER**.

g. Ma cousin**E** est médecin.

h. Mes oncles **SONT** fermiers.

12. Narrow listening: gapped translation

My name is **Andréa**. In my family there are **five** people. My **father** is called Christian. He is tall and **handsome**. He works as a **policeman**. He loves his job because it is **exciting**. My mother is an **accountant**. She does not **like** her job because it is **boring**. She wants to be a **nurse** because it is **rewarding,** and she is very **helpful**. My two **brothers** are students at **university**. They love it because it is **fun** and **interesting**. I am still a **student** in a secondary school. I hate school because it is **boring** and **difficult**.

TRANSCRIPT: Je m'appelle **Andréa**. Dans ma famille, il y a **cinq** personnes. Mon **père** s'appelle Christian. Il est grand et **beau**. Il travaille comme **policier**. Il adore son travail, car c'est **passionant**. Ma mère est **comptable**. Elle n'**aime** pas son travail, car c'est **ennuyeux**. Elle veut être **infirmière,** car c'est **gratifiant** et elle est très **serviable**. Mes deux **frères** sont étudiants à l'**université**. Ils adorent ça, car c'est **amusant** et **intéressant**. Je suis toujours **étudiante** en secondaire. Je déteste le collège, car c'est **ennuyeux** et **difficile.**

13. Listening Comprehension: listen and answer the questions about Valérie and Fernand

TEXT 1: Valérie		TEXT 2: Fernand	
What job does Valérie's father do?	Gardener	What job does his father do?	Lawyer
What does he think about his job?	Loves it - likes working outside/fresh air	What does he think about his job?	Doesn't like it - boring - repetitive
What job does Valérie's mother do?	Doctor	What job does his mother do?	Businesswoman
What does she think about her job?	She likes it - rewarding - she can help people	What does she think about her job?	Likes it - it's a bit difficult
What job does Valérie want to do one day?	Teacher	What job does Fernand want to do one day?	Singer
Why?	Work with kids - it's a creative job	Why?	Likes singing and playing guitar

TRANSCRIPT:
1. Salut, je m'appelle Valérie. Mon père est jardinier. Il adore son travail car il aime travailler dehors, en plein air. Ma mère est médecin dans un hôpital. Elle aime aussi son travail, car c'est gratifiant et elle peut aider les gens. Dans le futur, je veux être professeure car je veux travailler avec des enfants et c'est un travail créatif.
2. Salut, je m'appelle Fernand. Mon père est avocat et il n'aime pas son travail. Il dit que c'est ennuyeux et très répétitif. Ma mère est femme d'affaires. Elle aime assez son travail, mais c'est un peu difficile. Un jour, je veux être chanteur, car j'adore chanter et jouer de la guitare.

14. Narrow listening: fill in the grid

Name	Age	Character and appearance	Father's job	Mother's job	His/her ideal job
Jean-Marc	10	Short / strong	Worker	Teacher	Engineer
Marie	12	Tall / sporty	Hairdresser	Dentist	Lawyer
Pierre	15	Medium height / hardworking	Farmer	Housewife	Policeman
Andréa	13	Tall/ funny	Footballer	Actress	Doctor

TRANSCRIPT:
(1) Salut, je suis Jean-Marc et j'ai 10 ans. Je suis petit et fort. Mon père est ouvrier et ma mère est professeure. Un jour, je voudrais être ingénieur. **(2)** Salut, je suis Marie et j'ai 12 ans. Je suis grande et très sportive. Mon père est coiffeur et ma mère est dentiste. Un jour, je voudrais être avocate. **(3)** Salut, je suis Pierre et j'ai 15 ans. Je suis de taille moyenne et très travailleur. Mon père est fermier et ma mère est femme au foyer. Un jour, je voudrais être policier. **(4)** Salut, je suis Andréa et j'ai 13 ans. Je suis grande et marrante. Mon père est footballeur et ma mère est actrice. Un jour, je voudrais être médecin.

UNIT 9 – COMPARING PEOPLE'S APPEARANCE AND PERSONALITY

1. Multiple choice quiz: select the correct adjective

Alex (tall) **Rose** (short) **Pascal** (noisy) **Paul** (good-looking) **Amélie** (lazy) **Pierre** (unfriendly) **Marie** (strong) **Steven** (friendly) **Tristan** (serious) **Léa** (hard-working)

TRANSCRIPT:

1. Je m'appelle Alex et je suis grand.
2. Je m'appelle Rose et je suis petite.
3. Je m'appelle Pascal et je suis bruyant.
4. Je suis Paul et je suis beau.
5. Je m'appelle Amélie et je suis paresseuse.
6. Je m'appelle Pierre et je suis antipathique.
7. Je m'appelle Marie et je suis forte.
8. Je suis Steven et je suis sympathique.
9. Je suis Tristan et je suis sérieux.
10. Je m'appelle Léa et je suis travailleuse.

3. Complete with 'plus…que', 'moins…que' or 'aussi…que' as shown in the example

a. *Exemple: Ma mère est **plus** grande **que** mon père.*

b. Mon frère est **moins** sportif **que** moi.

c. Mon chat est **aussi** paresseux **que** mon chien.

d. Je suis **plus** fort **que** mon cousin.

e. Mon oncle est **moins** vieux **que** mon grand-père.

f. Mon meilleur ami est **aussi** petit **que** moi.

g. Mon oncle est **plus** gros **que** mon père.

h. Ma cousine Julie est **aussi** belle **que** ma cousine Léa.

5. Spot the differences and correct your text

a. Je suis plus grand que **mon père.**

b. Mon **frère** est aussi paresseux que moi.

c. Mon meilleur ami est **moins** bavard que moi.

d. Ma sœur est **aussi** belle que ma mère.

e. Mon chien est plus bruyant que mon **chat.**

f. Ma tante est **moins** vieille que ma grand-mère.

g. Ma mère est **plus** sportive que mon frère et moi.

2. Listening for detail: did you hear the masculine or the feminine form?

MASCULINE	FEMININE
ennuyeux	**ennuyeuse**
bavard	**bavarde**
paresseux	**paresseuse**
bruyant	bruyante
généreux	**généreuse**
grand	grande
sportif	sportive
sérieux	**sérieuse**
travailleur	travailleuse
amusant	**amusante**

TRANSCRIPT:

1. ennuyeuse	5. généreuse	8. sérieuse
2. bavarde	6. grand	9. travailleur
3. paresseuse	7. sportif	10. amusante
4. bruyant		

4. Listen and fill in the middle column as shown in the example with the missing information in English

Anne	*taller than*	*Philippe*
Sylvie	as short as	Alain
Jean	fatter than	Pierre
Paul	nicer than	Jules
Marie	less talkative than	Gérard
Caroline	lazier than	Léa
Julien	more hard-working	Julie
Philippe	more affectionate	Léon
Dylan	as stupid as	Samuel
Véronique	less sporty than	Serge

TRANSCRIPT:

Exemple: Je m'appelle Anne et je suis plus grande que Philippe.

1. Je m'appelle Sylvie et je suis aussi petite qu'Alain.
2. Je m'appelle Jean et je suis plus gros que Pierre.
3. Je m'appelle Paul et je suis plus sympa que Jules.
4. Je suis Marie et je suis moins bavarde que Gérard.
5. Je suis Caroline et je suis plus paresseuse que Léa.
6. Je m'appelle Julien et je suis plus travailleur que Julie.
7. Je suis Philippe et je suis plus affectueux que Léon.
8. Je suis Dylan et je suis aussi stupide que Samuel.
9. Je suis Véronique et je suis moins sportive que Serge.

 **THE LANGUAGE GYM**

6. Spot the missing words and write them in

Je m'appelle Jules. Dans ma famille **(il y a)** trois personnes. Nous sommes **(tous)** sportifs, mais mes parents sont plus sportifs que moi. Nous sommes **(aussi)** tous grands, mais je suis plus grand **(que)** mes parents. Nous sommes tous **(un)** peu gros, mais mon père est plus gros que **(ma)** mère et moi. **(Je)** suis le plus mince de ma famille! Nous sommes tous **(assez)** travailleurs, mais mes parents sont **(bien)** plus travailleurs que moi. Je suis un **(peu)** paresseux.

7. Faulty translation: spot the translation errors and correct them

ANSWERS:
My name is Jean-François. In my family there are **three** persons: my father, my **mother** and me. We are all very **fat**, but I am slimmer than my parents. We are all **friendly**, but my mother and I are more **serious** and hard-working than my father. We are all **tall**, but my father and my **uncle** are **shorter** than me. I am the **strongest** in the family.

TRANSCRIPT:
Je m'appelle Jean-François. Dans ma famille, il y a **trois** personnes: mon père, ma **mère** et moi. Nous sommes tous très **gros**, mais je suis plus mince que mes parents. Nous sommes tous **sympathiques**, mais ma mère et moi sommes plus **sérieux** et travailleurs que mon père. Nous sommes tous **grands**, mais mon père et mon **oncle** sont plus **petits** que moi. Je suis le plus **fort** de la famille.

8. Listen and complete the translation

	Person	Description
1	My father is…	taller than me
2	My mother is…	as pretty as me
3	My older brother is…	more muscular than me
4	My younger brother is…	slimmer than me
5	My sister is…	more hard-working than me
6	My uncle is…	shorter than me
7	My grandmother is…	more talkative than me
8	My best friend is….	less serious than me
9	My girlfriend is…	funnier than me
10	My dog is…	as calm as me

TRANSCRIPT:

1. Mon père est plus grand que moi.

2. Ma mère est aussi belle que moi.

3. Mon frère aîné est plus musclé que moi.

4. Mon frère cadet est plus mince que moi.

5. Ma sœur est plus travailleuse que moi.

6. Mon oncle est plus petit que moi.

7. Ma grand-mère est plus bavarde que moi.

8. Mon meilleur ami est moins sérieux que moi.

9. Ma petite amie est plus marrante que moi.

10. Mon chien est aussi calme que moi.

9. Listen, spot and correct the errors

a. Ma mère est plus **grande** que moi.

b. Mon père est plus travailleur que **moi**.

c. Mon frère aîné **est** plus fort que mon frère cadet.

d. Mon grand-père est plus **vieux** que ma grand-mère.

e. Je suis plus mince **que** mes parents.

f. Mes oncles sont **bien** plus vieux que mes parents.

g. Mes grands-parents maternels sont **aussi** vieux que mes grands-parents paternels.

h. Mes cousins **sont** plus riches que **nous.**

THE LANGUAGE GYM

10. Narrow listening: gapped translation

My name is Anthony and I am **twenty** years old. I am from Marseille, but I live in **London**. In my family we are **five** persons: my parents, my two **brothers**, Charles and Louis, and me. Charles is **taller**, more handsome and **stronger** than Louis, but Louis is more likeable, more intelligent and more **hard-working** than Charles. My **parents** are called Fernand and Pauline. They are both very **nice**, but my father is **stricter** than my mother. Moreover, my mother is more patient and less stubborn than my father. I am as **stubborn** as my father! I have a pet, a **duck** called Cacahuète. My parents say Cacahuète is as **noisy** as me.

TRANSCRIPT:

Je m'appelle Anthony et j'ai **vingt** ans. Je suis de Marseille, mais je vis à **Londres**. Dans ma famille, nous sommes **cinq** personnes: mes parents, mes deux **frères**, Charles et Louis, et moi. Charles est **plus grand**, plus beau et **plus fort** que Louis, mais Louis est plus aimable, plus intelligent et plus **travailleur** que Charles. Mes **parents** s'appellent Fernand et Pauline. Ils sont tous deux très **sympathiques**, mais mon père est **plus strict** que ma mère. De plus, ma mère est plus patiente et moins têtue que mon père. Je suis aussi **têtu** que mon père! J'ai un animal, un **canard** qui s'appelle Cacahuète. Mes parents disent que Cacahuète est aussi **bruyant** que moi.

11. Listen and write down what order you hear each chunk of text

6	My father is funnier than my mother
4	Gabrièle is prettier than Caroline
8	I am as generous as my mother
1	**My name is Pauline.**
5	Caroline is much nicer than Gabrièle
7	My father is less generous than my mother
2	I am twenty years old
9	However, my dog is as lazy as a sloth.
3	I live with my parents and my two sisters, Gabrièle and Caroline

TRANSCRIPT: Salut, je m'appelle Pauline et j'ai 20 ans. Je vis avec mes parents et mes deux sœurs, Gabrièle et Caroline. Gabrièle est plus belle que Caroline, mais Caroline est bien plus agréable que Gabrièle. Mon père est plus marrant que ma mère, mais mon père est moins généreux que ma mère. Moi je suis aussi généreuse que ma mère. Cependant, mon chien est aussi paresseux qu'un paresseux.

12. Answer the questions below about Éric

a. How old is he? **15**
b. Where does he live? **Calais**
c. How many people are there in the family? **Five**
d. Paul is **slimmer** and **sportier** than Jules
e. Jules is **taller** and **stronger** than Paul
f. Why does he prefer his father? **He is less strict**
g. He is as **stubborn** as his mother
h. Which of his pets is the most talkative? **The parrot**

TRANSCRIPT:

Salut, je suis Éric. J'ai 15 ans et je vis à Calais. Il y a 5 personnes dans ma famille. Mon frère Paul est plus mince et plus sportif que mon frère Jules. Cependant, Jules est plus grand et plus fort que Paul. Je préfère mon père car il est moins strict que ma mère. Je suis aussi têtu que ma mère. J'ai beaucoup d'animaux à la maison, mais mon perroquet est le plus bavard.

13. Listening slalom: follow the speaker from top to bottom and number the boxes accordingly

1	2	3	4
My mother is more (1)	My mother is as (2)	My mother is less (3)	My stepmother is (4)
affectionate than my father, (3)	**talkative than my father, (1)**	less hard-working than my mother, (4)	hard-working as my father, (2)
as sporty as (2)	as lazy as (3)	**as tall as (1)**	less generous than (4)
my father (4)	me (2)	my older sister (3)	**my younger sister (1)**
and less (3)	and much more	**and more (1)**	and as (2)
boring (4)	**annoying (1)**	unfriendly (2)	intelligent than (3)
as my younger sister (2)	her sisters (3)	than my aunt (4)	**than my brother (1)**

TRANSCRIPT: (1) Ma mère est plus bavarde que mon père, aussi grande que ma sœur cadette et plus pénible que mon frère. **(2)** Ma mère est aussi travailleuse que mon père, aussi sportive que moi et aussi antipathique que ma sœur cadette. **(3)** Ma mère est moins affectueuse que mon père, aussi paresseuse que ma sœur aînée et moins intelligente que ses sœurs. **(4)** Ma belle-mère est moins travailleuse que ma mère, moins généreuse que mon père et bien plus ennuyeuse que ma tante.

UNIT 10 – SAYING WHAT IS IN MY SCHOOLBAG/CLASSROOM

1. Multiple choice quiz: what items do they have?

		a	b	c
1	Raphaël	**a red pen**	a red pencil	a red rubber
2	Alexandra	a modern computer	modern furniture	**a modern classroom**
3	Romain	three books	**three pencil sharpeners**	three felt tip pens
4	Gabrièle	**a blue rubber**	a blue textbook	a blue pen
5	Jean-Louis	**some grey pencils**	some blue pencils	some green pencils
6	Dylan	**a black pencil case**	a black textbook	a black rubber
7	Marie-Hélène	an orange pencil sharpener	**an orange felt-tip pen**	an orange rubber
8	Tristan	**a red exercise book**	a red pencil	a red ruler
9	Caroline	a white ruler	**a white schoolbag**	a white dictionary

TRANSCRIPT:

(1) Je suis Raphaël et j'ai un stylo rouge. (2) Je suis Alexandra et ma classe est très moderne. (3) Je suis Romain et j'ai trois taille-crayons. (4) Je suis Gabrièle et j'ai une gomme bleue. (5) Je suis Jean-Louis et j'ai quelques crayons gris. (6) Je m'appelle Dylan et j'ai une trousse noire. (7) Je suis Marie-Hélène et j'ai un feutre orange. (8) Je m'appelle Tristan et j'ai un cahier rouge. (9) Je suis Caroline et j'ai un sac blanc.

2. Fill in the blanks

a. Dans ma **trousse**, j'ai deux crayons.

b. Dans mon **sac**, il y a deux **stylos**.

c. J'ai **besoin** d'un taille-crayon.

d. Mon **ami** Paul n'**a** pas de gomme.

e. Je n'ai ni **ciseaux**, ni **taille-crayon**.

f. Dans mon **sac**, il y a une **trousse**, deux **livres** et trois **cahiers**.

g. Dans ma **classe**, il y a le **bureau** du professeur et vingt **tables**.

4. Spot the differences and correct your text

1. Dans mon sac il y a une trousse **verte**, un livre d'**histoire**, un livre de géographie, deux cahiers **roses**, un dictionnaire et un **ordinateur portable**.

2. Mon ami Charles a des **crayons**, des stylos, un taille-crayon, **une gomme** et un tube de colle dans sa trousse. Il n'a pas **de règle**. Il n'a pas non plus de **compas**.

3. Mon amie Caroline a une trousse **rose**. Dans sa trousse, elle a deux **crayons**, **un stylo**, une règle et un **tube de colle**.

3. Listening for detail: tick which items the speaker does NOT have

Anne	a red pencil case
	two pens
	a gluestick
	a pencil sharpener
	a pencil
	six felt-tip pens
Sylvie	a green pencil case
	felt-tip pens
	two gluesticks
	three books
	a black pencil
	a white rubber
Véronique	a calculator
	a red ruler
	two books
	two pencils
	a rubber
	a fountain pen

TRANSCRIPT:

1. Je m'appelle Anne et dans mon sac j'ai une trousse rouge, deux stylos, six feutres et un tube de colle. Je n'ai ni de crayon, ni de taille-crayon, mais je n'en ai pas besoin.

2. Je m'appelle Sylvie et dans mon sac j'ai une trousse verte, deux tubes de colle, trois livres et un crayon noir. Je n'ai pas de feutres, ni de gomme blanche.

3. Je m'appelle Véronique. Dans mon sac, j'ai une calculatrice, deux livres, deux crayons et un stylo à plume. Cependant, je n'ai ni de règle rouge ni de gomme et j'en ai besoin.

5. Spot the missing words and write them in

Je m'appelle Raphaël. J'ai **(dix-sept)** ans et je vis à Grenoble, en France. Dans ma famille, **(il y a)** quatre personnes. Mon frère **(s')** appelle Serge. Dans ma classe, il y a deux **(tableaux),** et vingt-deux tables. Il y a aussi vingt-deux **(chaises)**. Ma classe est jolie, mais mon professeur est très ennuyeux. Dans ma trousse, je n'ai pas de crayon, **(ni)** de stylo, ni de règle, ni de gomme. Je n'ai **(rien)**. J'ai **(besoin)** de tout. À la maison, j'ai une souris **(blanche)**, elle est très marrante **(et)** elle s'appelle Pistache.

6. Faulty translation: spot and correct the errors

My name is Anthony. I am **15** years old and live in Valence, in France. In my family there are five persons. My **stepfather**, my mother, my brother, my **stepsister** and me. We also have a very funny **guinea pig**. In my classroom there are many things. There is a **whiteboard**, a computer and thirty **tables**. My classroom is very **big**. In my **pencil case** I have a blue pencil, a yellow **felt tip**, a new rubber and a white **ruler**. My friend Marc has **pencils** of all colours.

TRANSCRIPT:

Je m'appelle Anthony. J'ai **15** ans et j'habite à Valence en France. Dans ma famille, il y a cinq personnes. Mon **beau-père**, ma mère, mon frère, ma **demi-sœur** et moi. Nous avons aussi un **cochon d'Inde** très amusant. Dans ma classe, il y a beaucoup de choses. Il y a un **tableau**, un ordinateur et trente **tables**. Ma classe est très **grande**. Dans ma **trousse,** j'ai un crayon bleu, un **feutre** jaune, une gomme neuve et une **règle** blanche. Mon ami Marc a des **crayons** de toutes les couleurs.

8. Listen, spot and correct the errors

a. J'ai besoin d'**un** stylo.

b. Mon ami Paul a huit **crayons**.

c. J'ai **un** sac **blanc** et deux gommes.

d. Ma classe **est** petite, mais jolie.

e. Nous avons un animal **dans** ma classe, un cochon d'Inde.

f. Dans ma trousse, j'ai deux **règles**.

g. Ma sœur **a** besoin d'un ordinateur.

h. Mes cousins n'ont rien. Ils **ont** besoin de tout.

7. What do Louis and his friends need?

	Person	What they need
1	I need…	a calculator
2	My brother needs…	a yellow felt-tip
3	Sylvie needs…	a ruler
4	Naomi needs…	a pencil
5	Patricia needs…	a computer
6	Caroline needs…	a rubber
7	Raphaël needs…	a pencil sharpener
8	Michel needs…	a compass
9	Rose needs…	a red pen
10	Thérèse needs…	a white piece of paper

TRANSCRIPT:

1. Je m'appelle Louis et j'ai besoin d'une calculatrice.

2. Mon frère a besoin d'un feutre jaune.

3. Sylvie a besoin d'une règle.

4. Naomi a besoin d'un crayon.

5. Patricia a besoin d'un ordinateur.

6. Caroline a besoin d'une gomme.

7. Raphaël a besoin d'un taille-crayon.

8. Michel a besoin d'un compas.

9. Rose a besoin d'un stylo rouge.

10. Thérèse a besoin d'une feuille de papier blanc.

9. Narrow listening: gapped translation

My name is Simona and I am **Italian**. I am **14** years old and I live in the **south** of Italy. In my family, there are **six** people. I have a white **cat** and a black **rabbit**. In my **pencil case** I have a lot of things. I have a green **pen**, a yellow felt-tip pen, a **white** ruler, a grey compass and a white and blue **rubber**. My **schoolbag** is very big and **beautiful**. My best friend **is called** Lucie. She has only got one **thing** in her pencil case: a **pen**. In her house, she has a pet. It is a **talkative**, yellow and blue parrot that speaks and sings.

TRANSCRIPT:

Je m'appelle Simona et je suis **italienne**. J'ai **14** ans et je vis dans le **sud** de l'Italie. Dans ma famille, il y a **six** personnes. J'ai un **chat** blanc et un **lapin** noir. Dans ma **trousse** j'ai beaucoup de choses. J'ai un **stylo** vert, un feutre jaune, une règle **blanche**, un compas gris et une **gomme** blanche et bleue. Mon **sac** est très grand et **joli**. Ma meilleure amie **s'appelle** Lucie. Elle a seulement une **chose** dans sa trousse: un **stylo**. À la maison, elle a un animal. C'est un perroquet **bavard**, jaune et bleu qui parle et qui chante.

10. Listen and arrange the information in the same order as it occurs in the text

6	I don't get along with my stepfather.
4	In my family there are four people.
7	I like my school.
1	**My name is Alexandra.**
5	I love my mother.
8	But in my classroom, there isn't a computer.
2	I am twelve and live in Angers.
9	I have a brand-new school bag.
3	Angers is in the west of France.
10	…and I have many things inside.

TRANSCRIPT: Salut, je m'appelle Alexandra. J'ai 12 ans et je vis à Angers. Angers est dans l'ouest de la France. Dans ma famille, il y a 4 personnes. J'adore ma mère, mais je ne m'entends pas bien avec mon beau-père. J'aime mon collège, mais dans ma classe il n'y a pas d'ordinateur. J'ai un sac neuf et j'ai beaucoup de choses à l'intérieur.

11. Answer the questions below about Éric

a. Who is his favourite brother? **Jean-Paul**
b. What does his father do for a living? And his mother?
Father: fireman   Mother: nurse
c. What does he say about his school?
He likes it, but it is a bit boring sometimes
d. Why does he not like his classroom?
Small and no computer
e. What 3 (different) things are there in his schoolbag?
A pencil case, 2 books and 2 exercise books
f. What two things does he not have?
A rubber and a ruler

TRANSCRIPT: Salut, je m'appelle Éric et je suis d'Agen. J'ai deux frères, mais mon préféré s'appelle Jean-Paul. Mon père est pompier et ma mère est infirmière. Ils aiment tous les deux leur travail. J'aime mon collège, mais c'est un peu ennuyeux parfois. Je n'aime pas ma classe, car elle est très petite et il n'y a pas d'ordinateur. Dans mon sac, j'ai une trousse, deux livres et deux cahiers. Cependant, je n'ai ni de gomme, ni de règle et j'en ai besoin!

12. Listening slalom: follow the speaker from top to bottom and number the boxes accordingly

1	2	3	4
In my pencil case (1)	In his schoolbag (2)	In my schoolbag (3)	In her pencil case (4)
there are (3)	my sister has (4)	**I only have (1)**	my brother has (2)
a diary (2)	many things (3)	a few pencils (4)	**a pen (1)**
a few felt tip pens (4)	**a pencil (1)**	there are two books (3)	a pencil case (2)
some exercise books (2)	**a rubber (1)**	a calculator (4)	three exercise books (3)
a pencil sharpener (1)	a ruler (4)	a red pencil case (3)	a dictionary (2)
and two pens (4)	and a computer (3)	and his tablet (2)	**and scissors (1)**

TRANSCRIPT:

1. Dans ma trousse, j'ai seulement un stylo, un crayon, une gomme, un taille-crayon et des ciseaux.

2. Dans son sac, mon frère a un agenda, une trousse, des cahiers, un dictionnaire et sa tablette.

3. Dans mon sac, il y a beaucoup de choses. Il y a deux livres, trois cahiers, une trousse rouge et un ordinateur.

4. Dans sa trousse, ma sœur a des crayons, des feutres, une calculatrice, une règle et deux stylos.

 **THE LANGUAGE GYM**

UNIT 11 – TALKING ABOUT FOOD

1. Listen and fill in the gaps

a. J'adore **le chocolat**.

b. Raphaël aime beaucoup **le miel**.

c. Paul n'aime pas du tout **les légumes**.

d. Alexandre adore **le fromage**.

e. Mon père adore **la confiture** de fraises.

f. Ma mère déteste **les bananes**.

g. Mon frère adore **les crevettes**.

h. Ma sœur raffole de **poulet rôti** épicé.

i. Je déteste **les œufs**.

2. Mystery words: guess the words, then listen and see how many you guessed right

a. l'**eau**

b. le **miel**

c. l'**œuf**

d. la **viande**

e. le **poulet**

f. la **pomme**

g. le **pain**

h. le **riz**

3. Listening for detail: tick which food items Martine and Serge usually eat for breakfast

Martine	Du beurre
	Des tartines
	Un jus de fruits
	De la confiture
	Un œuf
	Du fromage
	Un café au lait
Serge	**Une saucisse**
	Un œuf
	Du riz
	Un café
	Du pain avec du miel
	Un jus d'orange
	Une banane

TRANSCRIPT:

1. Salut, je suis Martine. Pour le petit-déjeuner, je prends toujours des tartines, un œuf, du fromage et un jus de fruits.

2. Salut, je suis Serge. Pour le petit-déjeuner, normalement je prends une saucisse, un œuf, du pain avec du miel et un jus d'oranges.

4. Spot the differences and correct your text

a. J'adore les fruits, surtout les **fraises**.

b. Je déteste les légumes, surtout les **tomates**.

c. Je n'aime pas le poulet **rôti**.

d. J'aime beaucoup **le fromage**.

e. J'aime **un peu** les pâtes.

f. J'adore le jus **d'orange**.

g. La viande rouge est **mal**saine.

h. Le café est **dégoûtant**.

i. Les hamburgers sont **gras**.

j. Les légumes sont **délicieux**.

k. Les **carottes** sont croquantes.

l. Je n'aime pas **du tout** le lait.

 **THE LANGUAGE GYM**

5. Spot the missing words and write them in

Je m'appelle Fabrice. Qu'est-ce que tu **préfères** manger? Moi, j'adore **les** fruits de mer, donc j'aime **beaucoup** les crevettes et les calamars, car ils sont délicieux. J'adore aussi le poisson, car **c'est** savoureux et riche **en** protéines. J'adore **surtout** le saumon. J'aime **assez** le poulet rôti épicé. **De plus**, j'aime beaucoup les fruits, surtout les bananes **et les fraises**. Je ne supporte pas les légumes parce qu'ils **sont** dégoûtants.

6. Faulty translation: spot the translation errors and correct them

My name is Philippe. What do I like eating? I love **vegetables**, especially tomatoes. I **eat** them every day. My favourite vegetables are tomatoes and **spinach** because they are rich in vitamins. I also like **honey** because it is **sweet** and fruit because it is **healthy**. I hate **meat** and **fish**. They are rich in protein, but they are not **tasty**.

TRANSCRIPT:

Je m'appelle Philippe. Qu'est-ce que j'aime manger? J'adore les **légumes**, surtout les tomates. Je les **mange** tous les jours. Mes légumes favoris sont les tomates et **les épinards** car ils sont riches en vitamines. J'aime aussi **le miel** car c'est **sucré** et les fruits car c'est **sain**. Je déteste **la viande** et **le poisson**. Ils sont riches en protéines, mais ne sont pas **savoureux**.

8. Listen, spot and correct the spelling and grammar errors

a. J'**aime** les légumes, car ils sont sains.

b. J'**adore** les hamburgers.

c. Le poisson et la viande sont **savoureux**.

d. J'aime **assez** le jus d'orange.

e. Je mange **beaucoup** de poisson, car c'est riche en protéines.

f. Je n'aime pas **la** viande, car c'est gras.

g. J'adore **le** poulet rôti, car c'est savoureux.

h. J'**aime** beaucoup les calamars frits, même s'ils sont malsains.

7. Why do they like/dislike these foods?

	People/food	Reasons for likes/dislikes
1	I like fruit because	Healthy and sweet
2	My brother loves eggs	Rich in protein and tasty
3	Sylvie hates vegetables	Disgusting
4	Naomi dislikes crêpes	Too sweet
5	Pauline dislikes tomatoes	Not tasty
6	Caroline loves oranges	Bitter and healthy
7	Raphaël loves Indian food	Spicy and tasty
8	Ahmed doesn't eat pork	Religious reasons
9	Rose dislikes sausages	Greasy and unhealthy
10	Jean likes fish	Salty, tasty and healthy
11	Thérèse hates French fries	Salty and unhealthy
12	Sophie hates carrots	Hard and not tasty

TRANSCRIPT:

1. J'aime les fruits car ils sont sains et sucrés.
2. Mon frère adore les œufs car ils sont riches en protéines et savoureux.
3. Sylvie déteste les légumes car ils sont dégoûtants.
4. Naomi n'aiment pas les crêpes car elles sont trop sucrées.
5. Pauline n'aime pas les tomates car elles ne sont pas savoureuses.
6. Caroline adore les oranges car elles sont amères et saines.
7. Raphaël adore la nourriture indienne car c'est épicé et savoureux.
8. Ahmed ne mange pas de porc pour des raisons religieuses.
9. Rose n'aime pas les saucisses car elles sont grasses et malsaines.
10. Jean aime le poisson car c'est salé, savoureux et sain.
11. Thérèse déteste les frites car elles sont salées et malsaines.
12. Sophie déteste les carottes car elles sont dures et pas savoureuses.

9. Narrow listening: gapped translation

My name is Julien. What do I like to eat? I prefer **meat**, especially **pork**. I love it because it is **tasty**. I like burgers **a lot**. I love **sausages** too. I eat them with **French fries**. I also like fruit a lot because it is **sweet**. I don't like **vegetables**. I hate tomatoes and **carrots**. I also do not like **aubergines/eggplants** and **cucumbers**. They are **awful**. Moreover, I can't stand **eggs**. They are rich in protein and vitamins, but they are **disgusting**.

TRANSCRIPT:

Je m'appelle Julien. Qu'est-ce que j'aime manger? Je préfère la **viande**, surtout le **porc**. J'adore ça, car c'est **savoureux**. J'aime **beaucoup** les hamburgers. J'adore aussi les **saucisses**. Je les mange avec des **frites**. J'aime aussi beaucoup les fruits, car c'est **sucré**. Je n'aime pas les **légumes**. Je déteste les tomates et les **carottes**. Je n'aime pas non plus les **aubergines** et les **concombres**. Ils sont **horribles**. De plus, je ne supporte pas les **œufs**. Ils sont riches en protéines et vitamines, mais ils sont **dégoûtants**.

---

10. Listen and arrange the information in the same order as it occurs in the text

6	She likes lamb and pork.
4	She loves spinach and green beans.
8	He also loves French fries.
1	**In my family there are four people.**
5	My sister loves meat.
7	My father's favourite food is roast chicken.
2	We all like food and we eat a lot.
9	Me, I like cakes and sweets.
3	Vegetables are my mother's favourite food.
10	I also love honey, cos it's sweet and healthy.

TRANSCRIPT:

Dans ma famille, il y a 4 personnes. Nous aimons tous la nourriture et nous mangeons beaucoup. Les légumes sont la nourriture préférée de ma mère. Elle adore les épinards et les haricots verts. Ma sœur adore la viande. Elle aime l'agneau et le porc. La nourriture favorite de mon père est le poulet rôti. Il adore aussi les frites. Moi, j'aime les gâteaux et les bonbons. J'adore aussi le miel, car c'est sucré et sain.

---

11. Answer the questions below about Marie

a. How many people are in Marie's family? **Six**
b. What do her parents love? **Meat**
c. What does her mother hate? **Tomatoes**
d. What does her brother Raphael love?
Spicy roast chicken and French fries
e. What does her brother Jean love?
Fish and seafood
f. What does Marie love?
Bread with butter and jam
g. What does she hate? **Eggs**
h. Why? **She thinks they are disgusting**

TRANSCRIPT: Salut, je m'appelle Marie. J'habite à Saint-Malo et il y a 6 personnes dans ma famille. Mes parents adorent manger de la viande, mais par contre ma mère déteste les tomates. Mon frère, Raphaël, mange toujours du poulet rôti épicé avec des frites, il adore ça! Mon autre frère, Jean, adore le poisson et les fruits de mer. Et moi? J'adore le pain avec du beurre et de la confiture. Cependant, je déteste les œufs. À mon avis, ils sont dégoûtants.

---

12. Listening slalom: follow the speaker from top to bottom and number the boxes accordingly

1	2	3	4
I love (1)	I hate (2)	I can't stand (3)	I love (4)
chocolate (4)	**meat (1)**	spinach (2)	burgers (3)
and cakes (4)	sausages (3)	**because it is (1)**	and tomatoes (2)
or French fries (3)	because they are sweet (4)	because they are (2)	**tasty (1)**
and delicious (4)	disgusting. (2)	**and rich in protein. (1)**	because they are (3)
greasy (3)	**I eat it with salad (1)**	I prefer (2)	even if (4)
they're a bit unhealthy (4)	and unhealthy (3)	**or French fries (1)**	carrots (2)

TRANSCRIPT:

1. J'adore la viande car c'est savoureux et riche en protéines. J'en mange avec de la salade ou des frites.
2. Je déteste les épinards et les tomates car ils sont dégoûtants. Je préfère les carottes.
3. Je ne supporte ni les hamburgers, ni les saucisses, ni les frites parce qu'ils sont gras et malsains.
4. J'adore le chocolat et les gâteaux car ils sont sucrés et délicieux, même s'ils sont un peu malsains.

UNIT 12 – TALKING ABOUT FOOD – LIKES & DISLIKES

1. Listen and fill in the gaps

a. En général, je mange un **œuf** pour le petit-déjeuner.

b. Parfois, je mange des **fruits** pour le petit-déjeuner.

c. …mais je mange rarement des **gâteaux**.

d. Généralement, je mange du **riz** avec du poulet ou de la **viande** avec des légumes pour le déjeuner.

e. En général, je ne mange pas **beaucoup** pour le goûter.

f. De temps en temps, je prends du pain avec du **miel** pour le goûter.

g. Normalement, je mange de la **soupe** pour le dîner.

h. Parfois, je mange des **fruits de mer** ou du **poisson**.

2. Mystery verbs: guess the words, then listen and see how many you guessed right

a. Je ne **mange** pas beaucoup pour le dîner.

b. Je **prends** du pain avec de la confiture.

c. Je **bois** beaucoup d'eau.

d. Je **mange** de la viande avec de la salade.

e. J'**adore** les fruits.

f. Je **déteste** le poisson.

3. Listening for detail: tick which food items Serge usually eats for his various meals

Petit-déjeuner	Œufs Fruits **Fromage ✓ Pain ✓ Miel ✓**
Déjeuner	Viande Riz **Pâtes ✓ Poulet ✓ Soupe ✓**
Goûter	Confiture Gâteaux Lait **Tartine ✓ Nutella ✓**
Dîner	Soupe Légumes **Salade ✓ Fromage ✓ Viande ✓**
Boissons	Café au lait Lait **Eau ✓ Café ✓ Jus de pomme✓ Jus d'orange ✓**

TRANSCRIPT:

Salut, je m'appelle Serge. Normalement, je mange du pain avec du fromage ou du miel pour le petit-déjeuner. Ensuite, pour le déjeuner, je mange des pâtes avec du poulet et parfois de la soupe. L'après-midi, pour le goûter, je prends toujours une tartine avec du Nutella. J'adore le Nutella! Finalement, pour le dîner je mange une salade avec un peu de fromage et de la viande. J'adore la viande! Je bois du café, mais seulement le matin. Ensuite, pendant la journée je bois de l'eau ou du jus de pomme ou d'orange.

4. Spot the differences and correct your text

Pour le petit-déjeuner, en général, je mange **beaucoup**: une banane, deux ou trois **œufs**, des tartines avec du **jambon**, un jus **de pomme** et une tasse de **café au lait**. J'aime le café **sans sucre**.

A midi, en général, je mange seulement du riz avec du **poulet** ou des légumes et je bois **de l'eau minérale**. J'adore le poulet épicé, car c'est **savoureux** et c'est riche en **protéines**. **Souvent,** je mange des asperges. J'adore ça, car elles sont **amères** et riches en vitamines.

Pour le dîner, je ne mange pas beaucoup. D'habitude, je mange **des pâtes** et de la viande avec des légumes, et pour le dessert je prends **une glace** ou je **mange** des gâteaux.

5. Spot the missing words and write them in

Je m'appelle Fernand. En général, je ne mange pas **beaucoup** pour le petit-déjeuner. Seulement un œuf et **une tasse** de thé. J'aime le thé sucré, **avec** beaucoup de sucre. Parfois je bois du jus **d'ananas**. A midi, je mange du poulet **rôti** avec des légumes et je bois de l'eau **minérale**. Je mange beaucoup de légumes car ils sont **très** sains et délicieux. J'aimerais **manger** plus de crevettes, car j'adore ça! Après le collège, je prends deux tartines **avec du miel** et je bois une tasse de thé. J'adore le miel **car c'est** délicieux. Pour le **dîner,** je mange beaucoup. En général, je mange du riz, des fruits de mer **ou du poisson** avec des légumes et **pour le dessert,** un ou deux gâteaux.

6. Faulty translation: spot the translation errors and correct them

My name is Robert. In general, I don't eat much for **breakfast**. Only **a banana** and a **bit** of coffee.

At **noon**, usually I eat **meat** with **fries** and I drink mineral water. Sometimes, I eat roast **chicken**. I **never** eat burgers because they are **not healthy**. For dinner. I eat very **little**, usually **soup** or a salad.

TRANSCRIPT:

Je m'appelle Robert. En général, je ne mange pas beaucoup pour le **petit-déjeuner**, seulement une **banane** et un **peu** de café. À **midi**, d'habitude je mange de la **viande** avec des **frites** et je bois de l'eau minérale. Parfois, je mange du **poulet** rôti. Je ne mange **jamais de** hamburgers car ils ne sont **pas sains**. Pour le dîner, je mange très **peu**, généralement de la **soupe** ou une salade.

8. Listen, spot and correct the errors

Je ne mange pas **beaucoup** pour le petit-déjeuner, je prends seulement un œuf et une tasse de thé. J'aime **le** thé très sucré, avec beaucoup de lait. Parfois, je bois du **jus** d'ananas.

À **midi,** je mange du **poulet rôti** avec des légumes et je bois de **l'eau minérale**. Je mange beaucoup de légumes car ils **sont délicieux**.

Après le collège, pour le **goûter,** je **prends** une tartine **avec** de la confiture.

Pour le dîner, je prends **du** riz avec du poisson ou de la salade. Parfois, je mange une **glace à la fraise**.

7. Write in English what each person thinks about each food/drink *(items are mentioned in order)*

		Food	Opinion
1	**Jean**	Vegetables	Disgusting
		Yoghurt	Light
		Fruit	Healthy
		Peach	Juicy
		Food	**Opinion**
2	**Dylan**	Lemonade	Refreshing
		Seafood	Tasty
		Honey	Sweet
		French fries	Greasy

TRANSCRIPT:
1. Salut, je suis **Jean**. Je n'aime pas du tout les légumes, ils sont dégoûtants. Cependant, le yaourt est léger et les fruits sont sains. Les pêches, en particulier sont très juteuses.
2. Salut, je suis **Dylan**. J'adore boire de la limonade, c'est si rafraîchissant. Les fruits de mer sont savoureux et le miel est sucré. Je n'aime pas les frites car elles sont très grasses.

9. What do they have for lunch?

	What they eat and drink (3 details)
1	Meat, vegetables, a banana
2	Fish, seafood, ice cream
3	Pasta, chicken, an apple
4	A burger, French fries and a coke
5	A sandwich, an orange and a fruit juice
6	Sausages, salad, a cake

TRANSCRIPT:
1. Je mange toujours de la viande, des légumes et une banane pour le déjeuner.
2. Je mange du poisson, des fruits de mer et une glace.
3. Je mange des pâtes, du poulet et une pomme.
4. Pour le déjeuner, je prends un hamburger, des frites et je bois un coca.
5. Je prends un sandwich et une orange, et je bois un jus de fruits.
6. Pour le déjeuner, je mange toujours des saucisses avec de la salade et un gâteau.

10. Narrow listening: gapped translation

Usually, I don't eat **much** in the morning: a banana, one or two **eggs**, bread with **honey**, an **apple** juice and cup of coffee **without** sugar. It's a very **healthy** breakfast, rich in vitamins and **proteins**. At noon, I have **chicken** with **rice** and vegetables. I drink lemonade because it **refreshing** and delicious. At dinner I have a **fish** or **seafood** soup with some **vegetables**. I love ice-cream, because it is **sweet**.

TRANSCRIPT:

D'habitude, je ne mange pas **beaucoup** le matin: une banane, un ou deux **œufs**, du pain avec du **miel**, un jus de **pomme** et une tasse de café **sans** sucre. C'est un petit-déjeuner très **sain**, riche en vitamines et **protéines**. À midi, je prends du **poulet** avec du **riz** et des légumes. Je bois de la limonade car c'est **rafraîchissant** et délicieux. Pour le dîner, je prends une soupe de **poisson** ou de poulet avec quelques **légumes**. J'adore les glaces, car c'est **sucré**.

11. Listen and arrange the information in the same order as it occurs in the text

6	It is very healthy
4	At noon I eat a lot
8	I eat bread with honey or jam
1	**At breakfast I don't eat much**
5	I eat chicken with vegetables
11	I usually have fish or seafood
7	At around 4pm I have my snack
2	One or two eggs and a toast
9	It is delicious!
3	I also drink a coffee without sugar
10	I have dinner around 7.30pm
12	I drink 3 litres of water a day

TRANSCRIPT: Pour le petit-déjeuner, je ne mange pas beaucoup. Je prends un ou deux œufs avec une tartine. Je bois aussi un café sans sucre. À midi, je mange beaucoup. Je mange du poulet avec des légumes. C'est très sain. Vers 4 heures, je goûte. Je mange du pain avec du miel ou de la confiture. C'est délicieux! Je dîne vers sept heures et demie. Normalement je prends du poisson ou des fruits de mer. Je bois 3 litres d'eau par jour.

12. Answer the questions below on Éric

1. What 3 things does he eat at breakfast?
a. bread / b. honey / c. orange juice
2. How does he describe his breakfast? (two adjectives)
a. healthy / b. delicious
3. What does he usually have for lunch?
a. chicken / b. fish / c. seafood / d. salad
4. At what time does he have dinner?
6.45pm
5. What does he have for dinner?
a. vegetable soup / b. an apple

TRANSCRIPT:
Salut, je suis Éric. Pour le petit-déjeuner, normalement, je prends du pain avec du miel et un jus d'orange. J'adore mon petit-déjeuner car c'est sain et délicieux. Pour le déjeuner, je prends beaucoup de choses: du poulet et du poisson et parfois des fruits de mer avec de la salade. Pour le dîner, je mange assez tôt, à sept heures moins le quart. Je prends toujours une soupe de légumes et une pomme.

13. Listen to Paul talk about his family and fill in the grid

	Relationship to speaker	Starter	Main course	Dessert
Céline	Sister	Omelette	Boeuf bourguignon	Strawberry ice cream
Mélanie	Mother	Niçoise salad	Pork chop with vegetables	Chocolate éclair
Xavier	Grandad	Crudités salad	Roast chicken with mushrooms	Cake
Julien	Father	Seafood	Tuna fish with spinach	Crème brûlée

TRANSCRIPT: Salut, je m'appelle Paul. Dans ma famille il y a 5 personnes. Ma sœur **Céline** mange toujours des omelettes en entrée et ensuite du bœuf bourguignon. Son dessert favori, c'est la glace à la fraise. Ma mère, **Mélanie** prend généralement de la salade niçoise en entrée, et ensuite une côte de porc avec des légumes. Pour le dessert, elle prend un éclair au chocolat. **Xavier** est mon grand-père. Il prend toujours une salade de crudités en entrée. Ensuite, comme plat principal il prend du poulet rôti avec des champignons. Pour le dessert, normalement, il mange un gâteau. Mon père, **Julien** prend toujours des fruits de mer en entrée et du thon avec des épinards comme plat principal. Pour le dessert, il mange toujours une crème brûlée.

UNIT 13 – TALKING ABOUT CLOTHES AND ACCESSORIES

1. Listen and fill in the gaps

a. À la maison, **je porte** un pull.

b. À la plage, je porte un **maillot de bain**.

c. Au gymnase, je porte un **tee-shirt**.

d. Je ne porte jamais de **bottes**.

e. Quand il fait froid, je porte une **écharpe**.

f. Quand je sors en boîte, je porte une **chemise**.

g. Mon frère porte toujours des **chaussures** de sport.

h. Ma petite amie porte des **vêtements** élégants.

2. Mystery words: guess the words, then listen and see how many you guessed right

a. Une **écharpe**

b. Une **chemise**

c. Une **jupe**

d. Un **manteau**

e. Un **pull**

f. Un **costume**

g. Un **maillot de bain**

3. Listening for detail: tick the clothes David wears

Ce que je porte quand il fait froid	Une écharpe ✓
	Un pull
	Un manteau ✓
	Des bottes ✓
	Un maillot de bain
Ce que je porte quand je sors avec ma petite amie	Une chemise ✓
	Une ceinture
	Un pantalon ✓
	Des sandales
	Des chaussures élégantes
Ce que je porte quand je sors avec mes amis	Une veste de sport ✓
	Une jupe
	Un chapeau
	Un gilet
	Des chaussures de sport ✓
Ce que je porte quand je reste à la maison	Un pull
	Un tee-shirt ✓
	Des pantoufles ✓
	Un chapeau
	Un jean ✓

TRANSCRIPT:

Salut, je suis David et quand il fait froid, je porte une écharpe, un manteau et des bottes. Je n'aime pas du tout le froid. Quand je sors avec ma petite amie, je porte une chemise et un pantalon, mais si je sors avec mes amis, je porte une veste de sport et des chaussures de sport. Quand je reste à la maison, je porte un tee-shirt, un jean et des pantoufles.

4. Spot the differences and correct your text

Je m'appelle Alexandra. J'ai **dix-huit** ans. Je suis **très** sportive et j'ai des vêtements de toutes les couleurs et de **styles** différents.

Je préfère les vêtements de **bonne qualité,** mais pas trop **chers**. En général, à la maison je porte un **pull** ou un tee-shirt, **un jean** et des chaussures de sport ou des **pantoufles**.

Quand je vais au gymnase, je porte un **survêtement** et des chaussures de sport **noires**. J'ai **huit** survêtements différents. Ils **ne** sont **pas** de marque, mais cela m'est égal.

Quand je sors avec mes amis, je porte une veste de **sport**, un jean et des chaussures de sport.

Quand je sors avec mon petit **ami**, je mets des robes élégantes et **confortables** et mes **chaussures** préférées. Elles sont aussi **jolies** et confortables.

5. Spot the missing words and write them in

Je m'appelle Jean-Paul. J'ai dix-huit **ans**. Je suis **de** Cannes en France. Dans ma famille **il y a** quatre personnes et je m'entends bien avec tout le monde. Nous avons **trois** animaux: un chien, un perroquet très bavard et un poisson **rouge**.

J'adore acheter des vêtements, surtout des chaussures **de sport** et des tee-shirts de couleurs **et styles** différents. Je n'ai pas **beaucoup** de vêtements, mais j'aime beaucoup les vêtements **que j'ai**. J'adore les vêtements de marque **italienne**.

Quand il fait froid, **en général** je porte un manteau et un pantalon noir, **gris** ou bleu. Parfois, je porte une **veste** de sport. Quand il fait chaud, je porte des tee-shirts **sans** manches, un jean **et** des sandales. Ma nourriture **préférée**, c'est la pizza. J'adore aussi **le fromage** et les pâtes. Je déteste **les** légumes.

6. Faulty translation: spot the translation errors and correct them

I **love** clothes, especially sports clothes. I have many **tracksuits**. My favourite tracksuit is blue and **white**. I also have many sports shoes. At home, I usually wear a T-shirt, **old** jeans and **slippers**.
When I go out with my **friends**, if it's hot, I wear a T-shirt and **shorts**. If it's cold, I wear a **sports jacket** and my favourite jeans.

TRANSCRIPT:
J'**adore** les vêtements, surtout les vêtements de sport. J'ai beaucoup de **survêtements**. Mon survêtement favori est bleu et **blanc**. J'ai aussi beaucoup de **chaussures de sport**. À la maison, d'habitude je porte un tee-shirt, un **vieux** jean et des **pantoufles**.
Quand je sors avec mes **amis**, s'il fait chaud, je porte un tee-shirt et un **short**. S'il fait froid, je mets une **veste de sport** et mon jean favori.

8. Listen, spot and correct the errors

Je m'appelle Serge. J'ai quinze ans. Quand je vais **au** collège, je porte une chemise bleue, un **pantalon** bleu et des chaussures **blanches**.

À la maison, en général, je porte un tee-shirt, **un** jean et **des** pantoufles. J'ai **beaucoup** de tee-shirts et de jeans.

Quand je vais au gymnase, je porte un tee-shirt sans manches, **un short** et des chaussures **de** sport. Quand je vais au centre **commercial** avec **mes** amis, je porte une veste, une chemise, un pantalon noir ou **gris**, et des chaussures noires.

7. Write in English the clothing item/accessory and description

	Noun	Adjective
1	Skirt	Blue
2	T-shirt	Black
3	Suit	Grey
4	Earrings	Gold
5	Watch	Expensive
6	Skirt	Pretty
7	Shirt	White
8	Boots	Trendy

TRANSCRIPT:
1. Une jupe bleue.
2. Un tee-shirt noir.
3. Un costume gris.
4. Des boucles d'oreilles en or.
5. Une montre chère.
6. Une jolie jupe.
7. Une chemise blanche.
8. Des bottes branchées.

9. What are they wearing?

	Four details each
Pauline	a scarf, a jumper, a skirt, boots
Eva	a necklace, a T-shirt, jeans, trainers
Sylvain	a suit, a shirt, a tie and black shoes

TRANSCRIPT:
1. Mon amie Pauline porte toujours une écharpe, un pull, une jupe et des bottes.
2. Ma sœur Eva porte un collier, un tee-shirt, un jean et des chaussures de sport.
3. Mon cousin Sylvain est avocat. Pour aller au travail, il porte un costume, une chemise, une cravate et des chaussures noires.

10. Narrow listening: gapped translation

Usually, in the winter at home I wear a **jumper**, **old** trousers and **slippers**. In the summer, on the other hand, I wear a **t-shirt**, **shorts** and **flip-flops**. I have a lot of **sports clothes**, but also some **elegant** clothes. I like **branded** clothes, but it's very expensive, so I don't have **many**. When I go out with my friends or with my **girlfriend** in the **summer**, I wear a **trendy** T-shirt, **jeans**, trainers and **sunglasses**. However, in the **spring**, I wear a coat, Levi's jeans and **boots**.

TRANSCRIPT:

D'habitude, en hiver, à la maison je porte un **pull**, un **vieux** pantalon et des **pantoufles**. En été, par contre, je porte un **tee-shirt**, un **short** et des **tongs**. J'ai beaucoup de **vêtements de sport**, mais aussi des vêtements **élégants**. J'aime les vêtements **de marque** mais c'est très cher, donc je n'en ai pas **beaucoup**. Quand je sors avec mes amis ou avec ma **petite amie** en été, je porte un tee-shirt **branché**, un **jean**, des chaussures de sport et des **lunettes de soleil**. Cependant, au **printemps** je porte un manteau, un jean Levi's et des **bottes**.

11. Listen and arrange the information in the same order as it occurs in the text

3	I live in the south, in Provence
7	At school I wear a navy blue shirt
1	**My name is Gabrièle**
5	I have a yellow and blue parrot
10	with jeans and trainers
6	At home I wear a tracksuit
2	and I live in France
9	When I go out, I wear a pink T-shirt
4	I have three brothers and a sister
8	and black trousers

TRANSCRIPT: Je m'appelle Gabrièle et j'habite en France. J'habite dans le sud, en Provence. J'ai trois frères et une sœur. J'ai un perroquet jaune et bleu. Chez moi, je porte un survêtement. Au collège, je porte une chemise bleu marine et un pantalon noir. Quand je sors, je porte un tee-shirt rose avec un jean et des chaussures de sport.

12. Listen to André's description of himself and his family and answer the questions below in English

1. Where is he from? **Carcassonne**
2. How many siblings has he got? **2**
3. What are his favourite foods? (3 details)
Honey, ice cream and cakes
4. Why? **He likes sweet food**
5. What does he usually wear? (3 details)
(Trendy) t-shirt, shorts and flip-flops
6. What are his favourite shoes? (2) **Black trainers**
7. Who wears jeans and flip flops every day?
His older brother
8. Who wears elegant clothes? **His cousin Léa**

TRANSCRIPT: Salut, je suis André et je suis de Carcassonne. J'ai deux frères: un frère cadet et un frère aîné. Ce que je préfère manger, ce sont les glaces, le miel et les gâteaux. C'est parce que j'adore la nourriture sucrée. Normalement, je porte un tee-shirt branché, un short et des tongs. Mes chaussures préférées sont des chaussures de sport noires. Mon frère aîné porte un jean et des tongs tous les jours. Ma cousine Léa est avocate, elle porte toujours des robes et des costumes élégants.

13. Fill in the grid: what did they buy?

		Item bought	What for	Colour	Opinion	Price
1	**Léa**	Suit	Work	Navy blue	Elegant	50 euros
2	**Anne**	Trainers	Gym	White and green	Comfortable	45 euros
3	**Pierre**	Shirt	Go out with gf	Dark grey	Pretty	5 euros
4	**Marie**	High-heel shoes	Birthday party	Black and yellow	Not comfy	87 euros

TRANSCRIPT: (1) Salut, je suis Léa. Il y a deux jours, j'ai acheté un costume pour le travail. Il est de couleur bleu marine et très élégant. Il m'a coûté 50 euros. **(2)** Salut, je suis Anne. Hier, j'ai acheté des chaussures de sport pour aller au gymnase. Elles sont blanches et vertes et très confortables. Elles m'ont coûté seulement 45 euros. **(3)** Salut, moi c'est Pierre. Il y a trois jours, j'ai acheté une chemise pour sortir avec ma petite amie. Elle est de couleur gris foncé et très jolie. Elle m'a coûté 5 euros. Quelle affaire! **(4)** Salut, je suis Marie et la semaine dernière, j'ai acheté des chaussures à talons hauts pour une fête d'anniversaire. Elles sont noires et jaune, mais pas très confortables. Elles m'ont coûté 87 euros!

UNIT 14 – SAYING WHAT I AND OTHERS DO IN OUR FREE TIME

1. Complete with 'je joue', 'je fais' or 'je vais'

a. **Je joue** aux échecs.

b. **Je fais** de la musculation.

c. **Je joue** aux cartes.

d. **Je fais** de l'escalade.

e. **Je vais** à la piscine.

f. **Je vais** en boîte.

g. **Je vais** chez un ami.

h. **Je joue** avec mes amis.

2. Complete with the missing syllables

a. Je joue au te**nnis**.

b. Je fais de la rando**nnée**.

c. Je vais au centre spor**tif**.

d. Je vais en boî**te**.

e. Je fais du vé**lo**.

f. Je vais à la monta**gne**.

g. Je joue au badmin**ton**.

h. Je vais à la pla**ge**.

i. Je vais au par**c**.

j. Je fais de la nata**tion**.

3. Listening for detail: what activities does Aurélie do each day? Tick the correct one

Monday	**Cycling** ✓ Chess Rock climbing
Tuesday	Going to the mountain **Swimming** ✓ Going clubbing
Wednesday	**Going to the gym** ✓ Playing basketball Playing tennis
Thursday	Jogging **Homework** ✓ Horse riding
Friday	Skiing Weights **Chess** ✓
Saturday	Hiking Weights **Bike riding** ✓
Sunday	Swimming Weights **Fishing** ✓

TRANSCRIPT: Salut, je m'appelle Aurélie. Le lundi, je fais du vélo avec mon amie Andréa. Le mardi, je fais de la natation à la piscine. Le mercredi, je vais au gymnase avec mon ami Jean-François. Le jeudi, je reste à la maison et je fais mes devoirs. Le vendredi je joue aux échecs au collège. Le samedi, je fais du vélo à la montagne et le dimanche je vais à la pêche avec mon grand-père Claude.

4. Spot the intruders

Je m'appelle Thomas. Je suis ~~un~~ allemand. Je suis ~~très~~ sportif. Pendant mon temps libre, je fais ~~souvent~~ du sport. Mon sport préféré, c'est l'escalade ~~libre~~. Je fais de l'escalade **presque** tous les jours. Quand il fait mauvais, ~~en général~~ je reste chez moi et je joue aux échecs ou ~~je joue~~ aux cartes avec mon frère ~~cadet~~. J'aime aussi ~~beaucoup~~ faire de la natation. Je fais de la natation **presque** tous les week-ends à la piscine près de chez moi ~~maison~~.

5. Faulty translation: correct the translation
My name is Laura. I have **black** hair and I am very **intelligent** and talkative. I am not very sporty. I prefer to **watch TV**, play chess, play cards and go **to the park**. When the weather is nice, I like to go **fishing** and from time to time, I go to the **shopping centre** with my **mother**. I **never** go to the gym. It is very boring in my opinion. I prefer to go **biking**.

TRANSCRIPT:
Je m'appelle Laura. J'ai les cheveux **noirs** et je suis très **intelligente** et bavarde. Je ne suis pas très sportive. Je préfère regarder **la télé**, jouer aux échecs, jouer aux cartes et aller **au parc**. Quand il fait beau, j'aime aller **à la pêche** et de temps en temps je vais au **centre commercial** avec ma **mère**. Je ne vais **jamais** au gymnase. C'est très ennuyeux à mon avis. Je préfère faire du **vélo**.

6. What are their favourite hobbies?

1. Ninon	Swimming
2. Serge	Rock climbing
3. Laure	Skiing
4. Jean-Paul	Playing chess
5. Alexandre	Weight lifting
6. Lola	Going to the pool
7. Maurice	Going fishing
8. Xavier	Biking
9. Pascale	Reading

TRANSCRIPT:
1. Salut! Je m'appelle Ninon et mon passe-temps préféré, c'est la natation.
2. Bonjour, je suis Serge. Mon activité de loisirs favorite c'est l'escalade. J'adore ça!
3. Salut! Comment ça va? Je suis Laure et j'adore faire du ski.
4. Bonjour! Moi c'est Jean-Paul et pendant mon temps libre, je joue toujours aux échecs. C'est mon passe-temps favori!
5. Salut, je suis Alexandre et j'adore faire de la musculation.
6. Salut, je suis Lola et mon passe-temps favori c'est d'aller à la piscine.
7. Salut, je suis Maurice et je préfère aller à la pêche. C'est relaxant et divertissant. Bon pour moi en tout cas; mais pas pour les poissons.
8. Je m'appelle Xavier et pendant mon temps libre, je fais toujours du vélo.
9. Je m'appelle Pascale et quand j'ai le temps, je lis des livres. C'est mon passe-temps préféré!

9. Spot and correct the grammar/spelling errors

a. Je joue **aux** échecs.

b. Je vais **chez** mon ami.

c. Je fais **souvent** de l'escalade.

d. Je **ne** joue presque jamais au foot.

e. Je vais **au** centre sportif.

f. Je vais **en** boîte.

g. Quand il **fait** beau, je fais du footing.

h. Je fais du vélo **presque** tous les jours.

7. Spot the differences and correct your text

Je m'appelle Clive. Je suis **écossais**. J'adore faire de l'escalade. J'**en fais** tous les jours avec mes amis. C'est mon sport préféré! Parfois, je fais de l'**équitation**, du footing ou de la randonnée. Ce sont des sports passionnants. Je n'aime pas le **basket**, ni le foot. Ce sont des sports ennuyeux à mon avis. Je déteste aussi faire du **vélo**. Je fais du vélo très **rarement** au **parc** près de chez moi. **Une** fois par semaine, je vais en boîte avec mon **meilleur** ami, Glenn. **Nous aimons** danser.

8. Split sentences: listen and match

1. Je fais du vélo	a. montagne
2. Je joue au	b. beau
3. Je vais chez	c. au parc
4. Je vais à la	d. l'équitation
5. Quand il fait	e. basket
6. Je déteste faire de	f. tous les jours
7. Je ne fais jamais	g. avec mon ami Paul
8. Je vais souvent	h. de la randonnée
9. Je vais à la pêche	i. un ami

ANSWERS: 1f 2e 3i 4a 5b 6d 7h 8c 9g
TRANSCRIPT:
1. Je fais du vélo tous les jours.
2. Je joue au basket.
3. Je vais chez un ami.
4. Je vais à la montagne.
5. Quand il fait beau.
6. Je déteste faire de l'équitation.
7. Je ne fais jamais de la randonnée.
8. Je vais souvent au parc.
9. Je vais à la pêche avec mon ami Paul.

10. Mystery words: guess the words then check

a. Escalade

b. Cartes

c. Natation

d. Parc

e. Vélo

f. Ski

g. Pêche

h. Temps

i. Libre

11. Spot the missing words and write them in

Je m'appelle Luna, et je suis italienne. J'adore faire **du** vélo. Je fais du vélo avec **mes** amis. **C'est** mon sport préféré. J'**en** fais tous les jours. De temps **en** temps je fais de l'escalade, du footing, ou de la randonnée. Je n'aime pas du **tout** le tennis, ni **le** foot. Je déteste aussi **faire** de la natation. J'en **fais** très rarement car **c'est** fatigant. Deux fois **par** semaine, je vais en boîte avec ma **meilleure** amie Julia. J'adore danser dans **la** discothèque **avec** tous mes amis du collège.

12. Listen to Tristan talk about his friends and fill in the grid below in English

	Name	Age	Description	Favourite food	Favourite clothes	Favourite activity	How often they practise
1	Christophe	10	Tall + funny	Chicken + chips	Tracksuit	Football	Every weekend
2	Anthony	15	Short + lazy	Niçoise salad + fresh fish	White t-shirt	Basketball	Every Monday
3	Arnaud	12	Very tall + Strong	Fries with mayonnaise	Red shoes	Horseriding	Every day
4	Nico	14	A bit fat + very hard-working	Burgers + red meat	Yellow hat	Talking	A lot
5	Gilles	11	Tall + likeable	Salmon + soup	White and blue coat	Swimming	3 times a week

TRANSCRIPT:
Salut, je suis Tristan et je vais parler de mes amis. **(1)** Mon ami **Christophe** a 10 ans. Il est grand et marrant. Sa nourriture préférée, c'est le poulet avec des frites. Il porte toujours un survêtement car c'est confortable. Son sport favori, c'est le foot et il s'entraîne tous les week-ends. **(2)** Mon ami **Anthony** a 15 ans. Il est petit et très paresseux. Sa nourriture favorite c'est la salade niçoise avec du poisson frais. Il porte toujours un tee-shirt blanc. Son sport favori, c'est le basket et il en fait tous les lundis. **(3)** Mon ami **Arnaud** a 12 ans. Il est très grand et fort. Ce qu'il aime manger le plus, c'est les frites avec de la mayonnaise. Normalement, il porte des chaussures rouges. Son sport favori c'est l'équitation et il en fait tous les jours. **(4)** Mon ami **Nico** a 14 ans. Il est un peu gros et très travailleur. Sa nourriture préférée, ce sont les hamburgers et la viande rouge. Il porte toujours un chapeau jaune; c'est son favori. Il ne fait pas de sport, mais son activité favorite c'est parler et il le fait beaucoup. **(5)** Mon ami **Gilles** a 11 ans. Il est grand et aimable. Il adore manger du saumon et de la soupe. Son vêtement préféré, c'est un manteau blanc et bleu. Son sport favori c'est la natation et il en fait trois fois par semaine.

13. Narrow listening: gapped translation
My name is **Jean-Marc** and I am **17** years old. I am **French** and Corsican. I am an inhabitant from **Corsica**, the 'isle of beauty'. I live here with my **parents**, my two **brothers** and my **sister**. My parents are very **likeable** and **generous**. My brothers are very **annoying** and my sister is funny and **helpful**. What I like eating the most is **chicken** and **rice**. I also eat **salad** very often. In my free time, I do a lot of **sport**. I play **tennis** at school **every day**. I often do **weight lifting** at the gym near my house. Three times a week, I go **fishing** and from time to time I go to the **cinema** with my brothers. Besides sport, I also play **guitar** and go to guitar **lessons** once a week. I love **music**. Goodbye!

TRANSCRIPT:
Mon nom est **Jean-Marc** et j'ai **17** ans. Je suis **français** et corse. Je suis un habitant de **la Corse**, 'l'île de beauté'. Je vis ici avec mes **parents**, mes deux **frères** et ma **sœur**. Mes parents sont très **aimables** et **généreux**. Mes frères sont très **pénibles** et ma sœur est amusante et **serviable**. Ce que j'aime manger le plus, c'est le **poulet** et le **riz**. Je mange aussi très souvent de la **salade**. Pendant mon temps libre, je fais beaucoup de **sport**. Je joue au **tennis** au collège **tous les jours**. Souvent, je fais de la **musculation** au gymnase près de chez moi. Trois fois par semaine, je vais **à la pêche** et de temps en temps je vais au **cinéma** avec mes frères. En plus du sport, **je joue de la guitare** et je vais à des **cours de guitare** une fois par semaine. J'adore la **musique**. Au revoir!

UNIT 15 – TALKING ABOUT WEATHER AND FREE TIME

1. Listen and fill in the gaps

a. Quand j'ai le **temps**, je joue aux échecs.

b. Quand le ciel est **dégagé**, je fais du vélo.

c. Quand il fait **beau**, je fais du footing.

d. Quand il fait **chaud**, je vais à la plage.

e. Quand il **pleut**, je vais au centre commercial.

f. Pendant la **semaine**, je ne fais pas de sport.

g. Quand il **neige**, je ne fais pas de vélo.

h. Quand il y a de l'**orage**, je reste à la maison.

i. Quand il fait **mauvais**, je fais mes devoirs.

2. Mystery words: guess the words, then listen and see how many you guessed right

a. La **neige**

b. Il fait **chaud**

c. Le **vent**

d. Le **soleil**

e. **Dégagé**

f. Quand il **pleut**

g. Il y a des **nuages**

h. Il fait **froid**

3. Listening for detail: tick the activities these three people do at the weekend

1	Paul	Goes jogging Goes to the shopping centre **Goes horse riding** ✓ **Does his homework** ✓ **Goes clubbing** ✓
2	Anne	**Goes swimming** ✓ **Goes to the shopping centre** ✓ Goes to the sports centre Plays on the computer **Goes to restaurant** ✓
3	Caroline	**Goes jogging** ✓ Goes to the shopping centre Goes horse riding **Plays chess** ✓ **Goes to her friend's house** ✓

TRANSCRIPT:

(1) Salut, je suis Paul. Pendant mon temps libre je fais de l'équitation car j'adore les chevaux et je fais aussi mes devoirs. Le week-end, je vais en boîte.

(2) Salut, je suis Anne. Pendant mon temps libre, j'adore faire de la natation. Je vais aussi au centre commercial avec mes amis et au restaurant avec ma famille.

(3) Salut, je m'appelle Caroline et pendant mon temps libre je fais toujours du footing. Je joue aussi aux échecs et je vais chez mon ami Simon.

4. Fill in the blanks with the appropriate words

Qu'est-ce que je fais pendant mon temps libre? Beaucoup de choses. Quand il fait beau, je vais toujours au **parc**. J'aime **courir**, donc je fais du **footing**, seul ou avec mon **chien**. Mon chien aime aussi courir. Par ailleurs, j'**adore** faire de l'escalade et de la **randonnée**. De temps en temps, quand il ne **pleut** pas, je fais de la randonnée dans le bois près de chez moi. J'habite à la **campagne**. Quand le ciel est **dégagé** et qu'il fait **chaud**, je vais à la **plage**. J'adore la **natation** et bronzer au **soleil**.

Quand il fait **mauvais**, surtout quand il **pleut**, je reste à la maison. Je surfe sur **internet**, je fais mes devoirs, je joue aux **échecs** avec mon frère aîné ou je lis un **roman**. J'adore passer du temps en **famille**.

5. Spot the missing words and write them in

Je m'appelle Thomas. Je suis **de** Suisse. J'ai dix-huit **ans**. Quand il **fait** chaud et que le ciel est dégagé, je vais **à** la piscine et je **fais** de la natation. Je **vais** aussi parfois à la pêche avec **mon** père sur **son** bateau. C'est **un** peu ennuyeux, mais cela **me** plaît. Le **soir,** je vais en boîte avec mes amis. Quand je vais **en** boîte, en général, je porte **un** tee-shirt et un jean. Mon amie **s'appelle** Sophie. Elle est sympathique **et** intelligente. **Quand** il fait mauvais et qu'il pleut, **elle** reste toujours à la maison et fait **ses** devoirs.

6. Faulty translation: correct the errors

In my free time, I do lots of **things**. First of all, I love to sing and to play the guitar. Moreover, I like to buy shirts, **t-shirts** and **trainers**. I love to go shopping when it is **stormy**. When the weather is **nice**, I like to go to the **park** or hiking in the **countryside.** When it is **hot**, I prefer to go to the beach or the **lake** to swim. When it is **windy**, I go windsurfing or sailing. In the winter, when it **snows**, I quite like to go to the **mountain** with my family. I love **skiing.**

Transcript: Pendant mon temps libre, je fais beaucoup de **choses**. Premièrement, j'adore chanter et jouer de la guitare. De plus, j'aime acheter des chemises, des **tee-shirts** et des **chaussures de sport**. J'adore faire les magasins quand il y a de **l'orage**. Quand il fait **beau**, j'aime aller au **parc** ou faire de la randonnée **à la campagne**. Quand il fait **chaud**, je préfère aller à la plage ou **au lac** pour nager. Quand il y a du **vent**, je fais de la planche à voile ou de la voile. En hiver, quand il **neige**, j'aime assez aller à la **montagne** avec ma famille. J'adore **skier**.

8. Listen, spot and correct the spelling and grammar errors

Je m'appelle Patrice. Je suis **de** Biarritz, mais je vis à Nice, dans **le** sud-est de la **France**. Je suis grand et **mince**. Je vis avec **mes** parents et mon frère **aîné**, Georges. Je m'entends très bien avec mes **parents**. Nous passons **beaucoup** de temps **ensemble**. J'aime beaucoup jouer aux échecs avec mon père et **aux** cartes avec ma mère. Je passe aussi beaucoup de temps avec **mon frère**. Nous **faisons** du sport ensemble: du footing, de la natation et de la **musculation**. Le week-end, nous allons **en** boîte ensemble.

7. Write in English what each person thinks about different types of weather

	Opinion	Weather	Activity
1	**Loves**	**Hot**	**Beach**
2	Likes	Nice weather	Jogging
3	Loves	Wind	Sailing
4	Loves	Storms	Watch TV
5	Hates	Cold	Shopping
6	Dislikes	Bad weather	Homework
7	Loves	Clear sky	Hiking
8	Likes	Cloudy	Sports centre

TRANSCRIPT:
1. Exemple: J'adore la chaleur. Quand il fait chaud, je vais à la plage.
2. J'aime quand il fait beau, car je peux faire du footing.
3. J'adore le vent, car c'est parfait pour faire de la voile.
4. J'adore les orages, car je peux rester à la maison et regarder la télé.
5. Je déteste le froid. Quand il fait froid, je vais faire les magasins au centre commercial.
6. Quand il fait mauvais, je n'aime pas cela, car je dois faire mes devoirs à la maison.
7. Quand le ciel est dégagé, j'adore cela, car je peux faire de la randonnée à la montagne.
8. J'aime quand il y a des nuages, car je vais au centre sportif avec mes amis.

9. Sentence puzzle: rewrite the sentence in the correct order, then listen to check your answers

a. Quand il fait froid, je reste à la maison.
b. Quand il fait mauvais, je vais faire les magasins au centre commercial.
c. Quand il pleut, mon père et moi jouons aux échecs.
d. Quand il fait chaud, on va à la plage.
e. Quand il fait beau, nous allons faire une promenade dans le parc.
f. Quand il neige, nous faisons du ski à la montagne.
g. Quand le ciel est dégagé, je fais du footing avec mon chien.

10. Listen and arrange the information in the same order as it occurs in the text

6	It's a boring job
4	I am a student
8	When it's hot I go to the beach
1	**I live in Dakar, in Sénégal**
5	In the summer I work in a shop
11	When it's windy
7	I love sport
2	I am tall and muscular
9	I love to swim
3	I am funny and friendly
10	I also enjoy scuba diving
12	I go sailing

TRANSCRIPT:

Salut, j'habite à Dakar, au Sénégal. Je suis grand et musclé. Je suis marrant et sympathique. Je suis étudiant. En été, je travaille dans un magasin. C'est un travail ennuyeux. J'adore le sport. Quand il fait chaud, je vais à la plage. J'adore nager. J'aime aussi faire de la plongée. Quand il y a du vent, je fais de la voile.

11. Listen to Denise and answer the questions below in English

1. Which city is she from? In which country is this located? **Nouméa, New Caledonia**
2. Where does she live?
Calais (in the north of France)
3. What is the weather like? **Cloudy and often rains**
4. What does she do when the weather is bad? (three details)
a. Stays at home
b. Watches TV
c. Plays on the computer
5. What does she do when the weather is nice? (three details)
a. Jogging
b. Goes to the park
c. Goes to town centre with friends

TRANSCRIPT:

Salut, je suis Denise! Je suis de Nouméa, en Nouvelle Calédonie, mais je vis à Calais, dans le nord de la France. Ici, il y a des nuages et il pleut souvent. Quand il fait mauvais, je reste à la maison et je regarde la télé ou je joue sur mon ordinateur. En revanche, quand il fait beau, je fais du footing, je vais au parc ou je vais en centre-ville avec mes amis.

12. Listen to Anne talk about her family and then fill in the grid

	I (Anne)	My mother	My father	My sister
Personality	Funny	Likeable	Hard working	Lazy
Physique	Tall	Very pretty	Muscly	Skinny
Favourite clothes	Old jeans	White dress	Black shirt	Pink T-shirt
What they do in good weather	1. Jogging 2. Going to park	1. Walk the dog 2. Play tennis	1. Horse-riding 2. Go to the pool	1. Go to the beach 2. Sunbathe
What they do in bad weather	1. Play chess 2. Watch tv	1. Watch tv series 2. Surf on internet	1. Play cards 2. Work	1. Reads books 2. Listen to music
What they do when it is hot	Go to beach	Go to the pool	Stay at home	Go to the park

TRANSCRIPT:

Salut, je m'appelle **Anne**. Je suis marrante et grande. Mon vêtement favori, c'est mon vieux jean. Il est vieux, mais très confortable. Quand il fait beau, je fais du footing et je vais au parc. Quand il fait mauvais, je joue aux échecs et je regarde la télé. Quand il fait chaud, je vais toujours à la plage.

Ma mère est aimable et très belle. Elle porte toujours une robe blanche. C'est sa robe préférée. Quand il fait beau, elle va faire une promenade avec le chien. Elle joue aussi au tennis. Quand il fait mauvais, elle regarde des séries à la télé ou surfe sur internet. Quand il fait chaud, elle va à la piscine.

Mon père est travailleur et musclé. Il aime porter une chemise noire. Quand il fait beau, il fait de l'équitation et il va à la piscine; mais quand il fait mauvais il joue aux cartes ou fait son travail. Il n'aime pas la chaleur, ainsi, quand il fait chaud il reste à la maison.

Ma sœur est paresseuse et mince. Elle porte toujours un tee-shirt rose. C'est son préféré. Quand il fait beau, elle va toujours à la plage et bronze au soleil. En revanche, quand il fait mauvais, elle préfère lire des livres et écouter de la musique. Quand il fait chaud, elle va au parc.

UNIT 16 – TALKING ABOUT MY DAILY ROUTINE

1. Listen and fill in the gaps

1. Il est six heures et **quart**.

2. Il est **une** heure.

3. Il est six heures et **demie**.

4. Je me lève vers **six** heures.

5. Je sors de chez moi à **sept** heures et demie.

6. Je vais au collège à huit heures **moins** le quart.

7. Je déjeune à **midi**.

8. Je fais mes devoirs **vers** cinq heures.

9. Je me couche vers neuf **heures**.

2. Multiple choice quiz: Daily routine times

	a	b	c
1	6:00 am	**7:00 am**	9:00 am
2	10:00 am	10:05 am	**10:10 am**
3	2:45 pm	**3:45 pm**	2:15 pm
4	6:15 pm	**5:45 pm**	6:05 pm
5	11:05 am	10:55 am	**10:25 am**
6	**2:30 pm**	2:15 pm	2:20 pm
7	3:15 pm	2:45 pm	**2:35 pm**
8	12 pm	**12 am**	1 pm
9	7:20 am	7:10 am	**7:50 am**
10	8:15 am	**7:45 am**	2:35 am

TRANSCRIPT:

1. Je me lève tous les jours à 7:00 am.
2. J'ai récréation à 10:10 am.
3. Je sors du collège à 3:45 pm.
4. Je regarde la télé à 5:45 pm.
5. Je discute avec mes amis à 10:25 am.
6. Les cours finissent à 2:30 pm.
7. Je prends le bus à 2:35 pm.
8. Mon père se couche à minuit.
9. Mon ami se lève à 7:50 am.
10. Mon ami sort de chez lui à 7:45 am.

3. Which of the following times do you hear in the text? Tick the ones you hear

Not mentioned:

4:00   6:20   7:30   8:05   12:10

Mentioned:

6:00 ✓   **6:15** ✓   **7:20** ✓   **8:25** ✓   **12:00** ✓

TRANSCRIPT:

Salut, je m'appelle David. Tous les jours, je me réveille à 6:00 am et ensuite je me lève à 6:15 am. Je prends mon petit-déjeuner dans la cuisine à 7:20 am. Ensuite, je sors de chez moi et je vais au collège. J'arrive à 8:25 am. Après mes cours du matin, je déjeune à midi (12:00 pm).

4. Write out the times below, then listen to check if they are correct

1. 8:15 = huit heures et quart
2. 7:45 = huit heures moins le quart
3. 9:20 = neuf heures vingt
4. 6:40 = sept heures moins vingt
5. 11:30 = onze heures et demie
6. 9:25 = neuf heures vingt-cinq
7. 10:35 = onze heures moins vingt-cinq
8. Midnight = minuit
9. Midday = midi

5. Spot the differences and correct your text

Je m'appelle Renaud. Je suis **belge**. Je me **lève** toujours vers six heures et demie. Ensuite, je me douche et je **me peigne** après. Je ne mange pas **beaucoup** le matin, mais mon frère Valentin mange des céréales dans la salle à manger avec **mon père**. Je vais au collège **à pied** vers sept heures et quart. Je rentre à la maison vers **trois** heures et **demie** et ensuite je me détends un peu. En général, **j'écoute** de la musique dans le salon. Après, je surfe sur internet, je regarde une série sur Netflix ou des vidéos sur TikTok dans ma **chambre**. Ensuite, à **sept** heures, je prépare le repas avec ma mère dans la cuisine. J'adore préparer des **gâteaux** car ils sont **délicieux**. Je me couche tard, vers **minuit**.

6. Spot the missing words and write them in

Je m'appelle Fabien. Je suis **de** Gibraltar. J'ai un chien **à** la maison. Là où j'habite, il y a **beaucoup** de singes. Je **me** lève toujours tôt, à six heures **et** quart. Ensuite, je vais au gymnase et je **fais** du sport. Je me douche **et** je rentre à la maison. Mon frère Joël **est** très paresseux. Il se lève à sept heures. Joël **ne** joue pas au foot et il ne fait jamais de sport. Ainsi, il est **très** gros. Le soir, **je lis** des bandes dessinées dans ma chambre ou j'écoute de la musique. **Pendant** la semaine, quand je rentre à la maison, je fais **mes** devoirs dans le salon avec ma mère. J'aime ma mère, car **elle** est très intelligente et **m'**aide toujours. Finalement, je me couche à neuf heures, dans **ma** chambre.

7. Faulty translation: correct the translation

My name is Akiko, I am **Japanese**. My daily routine is **very** simple. In general, I get up very early, **around** 5:00. I go jogging and then I shower and have breakfast with my mother around **6:45**. Normally, I eat an egg or two and have some **bread**. Around 8:00 I leave my house and go to school **by bike.** I come back home from school at around **4:30**. Then, I rest a bit. In general, I watch **a movie** and I chat with my friends on **Whatsapp**. From 6:00 to 8:00 I do my homework. I **hate** doing my homework! Then, at around **7:45**, I have dinner with my family. I don't eat a lot. Only a salad and some **chicken** or fish. Afterwards, I play on my Playstation until **11:00**. Finally, I go to bed.

TRANSCRIPT: Je m'appelle Akiko, je suis **japonaise**. Ma routine journalière est **très** simple. En général, je me lève très tôt, **vers** 5:00. Je fais du footing et puis je me douche. Ensuite, je prends mon petit-déjeuner avec ma mère vers **6:45**. Normalement, je mange un œuf ou deux et je prends un peu de **pain**. Vers 8:00, je sors de chez moi et je vais au collège **en vélo**. Je rentre à la maison vers **4:30**. Ensuite, je me repose un peu. En général, je regarde **un film** et je tchatte avec mes amis sur **Whatsapp**. De 6:00 à 8:00, je fais mes devoirs. Je **déteste** faire mes devoirs! Puis, vers **7:45**, je dîne avec ma famille. Je ne mange pas beaucoup. Seulement une salade et du **poulet** ou du poisson. Ensuite, je joue à la Playstation jusqu'à **11:00**. Finalement, je me couche.

8. Listen and note down in English what Caroline does at each time

	Activity
6:30	Shower
7:15	Goes to school (by bike)
8:00	Has her first lesson of the day
9:15	She eats a sandwich
3:30	Plays basketball (with friends after school)
3:45	Does her homework
6:30	Goes to the gym
10:00	Watches television
11:00	Goes to bed

TRANSCRIPT: Salut, je suis Caroline.

Tous les jours, à 6:30 je me douche.

Ensuite, je vais au collège en vélo à 7:15. Mon premier cours commence à 8:00. À 9:15, pendant la récréation, je mange un sandwich. Après le collège, à 3:30, je joue au basket avec mes amis. À 3:45, je rentre à la maison et je fais mes devoirs dans ma chambre. Ensuite, à 6:30 je vais au gymnase. Finalement, à 10:00 je regarde la télé, et après je me couche à 11:00.

9. Listen, spot and correct the errors

Je m'appelle Alex. Je suis de Belle-Île-en-Mer. J'ai deux **chevaux** chez moi. Je **me** lève toujours tôt, à six heures **et** quart. Ensuite, je vais au centre sportif et je joue **au** badminton. Je me **douche** quand je rentre à la maison, mais mon frère Joël **est** très paresseux et ne **se** douche jamais. Il se lève à sept heures. Joël ne joue jamais **au** foot, et ne fait jamais de sport. Par conséquent, il **est** très gros. **Pendant** la semaine, quand je rentre chez moi, je fais **mes** devoirs dans le salon avec ma mère. J'aime ma mère, car elle est très intelligente et **m'**aide toujours. Finalement, je me couche à neuf heures.

10. Listening slalom: follow the speaker and number the boxes accordingly

1. Myriam	2. René	3. Tristan	4. Sophie
Je me réveille. (1)	Je me lève. (2)	Je me douche. (3)	Je sors du collège. (4)
Ensuite, je vais au gymnase. (3)	**Ensuite, je me lève. (1)**	Ensuite, je prends mon petit-déjeuner. (2)	Ensuite, je m'habille. (4)
Après, je rentre à la maison, (4)	Après, je m'habille, (2)	Après, je prépare mon sac, (3)	**Après, je me douche, (1)**
et ensuite, je sors de chez moi. (1)	et ensuite, je sors de chez moi. (3)	et ensuite, je me peigne. (2)	et ensuite, je me repose un peu. (4)
Finalement, je fais mes devoirs. (2)	Finalement, je m'habille. (4)	**Finalement, mon père me conduit au collège en voiture. (1)**	Finalement, je vais au collège. (3)

Literally no room on this page for a transcript, désolé! Ronan ☺

11. Narrow listening: gapped translation

My name is Pierre. I am **12**. I am from **Paris**. My daily routine is very **simple**. In general, I get up **early**, at around 5:30 am. Then, I shower and **I put on** my uniform. **Then**, I have breakfast with my brothers. Then I brush **my teeth** and prepare my **rucksack**. At around **quarter** past seven, I leave home and I go to school. I **return** home at around four. After this, I rest **a bit**. Generally, I read my **favourite** magazines. From six to **seven**, I do my homework. Then, at eight, I have **dinner**. I don't eat **meat**. Finally, I read a **book** or I surf on the **internet**. Finally, I **go to bed** at 10:35 pm.

TRANSCRIPT: Je m'appelle Pierre. J'ai **12** ans. Je suis de **Paris**. Ma routine journalière est très **simple**. En général, je me lève **tôt**, vers cinq heures et demie. Ensuite, je me douche et **je mets** mon uniforme. **Après**, je prends le petit-déjeuner avec mes frères. Ensuite, je **me brosse les dents** et je prépare mon **sac**. Vers sept heures **et quart**, je sors de chez moi et je vais au collège. Je **rentre** chez moi vers quatre heures. Après cela, je me repose **un peu**. Généralement, je lis mes magazines **favoris**. De six à **sept** heures, je fais mes devoirs. Ensuite, à huit heures, je **dîne**. Je ne mange pas de **viande**. Ensuite, je lis un **livre** ou je surfe sur **internet**. Finalement, **je me couche** à dix heures trente-cinq.

12. Fill in the grid: what do the different people do?

	Me (Valérie)	My mother	My father	My sister
At 7:30	I shower	prepares breakfast	shaves	gets dressed
At 8:15	I go to school by bike	goes to work	arrives at work	goes to university
At 12:00	I have chicken with fries	has a salad	has a steak with vegetables	goes to the gym
From 3:00 to 4:00	I play basketball with friends	comes back home (on horse)	stays at the office	goes to her biology lesson
From 6:00 to 8:00	I do my homework	goes to the sports centre	comes back home (by bus)	plays on the computer
From 8:30 to 11:00	I surf on the internet	watches a series on Netflix	watches videos on YouTube	chats with her friend, Philippe

TRANSCRIPT: Salut! Je m'appelle **Valérie** et j'habite à la campagne. Tous les jours, je me douche à 7:30. Ensuite, je sors de chez moi et je vais au collège en vélo à 8:15. À midi, je mange du poulet avec des frites. Plus tard, de 3 à 4 heures, je joue au basket avec mes amis. À 6 heures, je fais mes devoirs pendant 2 heures et après à 8:30, je surfe sur internet et je regarde des vidéos de danse sur Tiktok. **Ma mère** prépare le petit-déjeuner à 7:30 et ensuite va au travail à 8:15. À midi, elle mange une salade. À 3 heures, elle rentre à la maison à cheval. Après, elle va au centre sportif à 6 heures. Finalement, à 8:30 elle se repose en regardant une série sur Netflix. **Mon père** se réveille à 7 heures et se rase à 7:30. Il arrive tôt au travail, à 8:15. À midi, il mange un steak avec des légumes. De 3 à 4 heures, il reste au bureau. Après 6 heures, il rentre à la maison en bus. Avant de dormir, de 8:30 à 11 heures, il regarde des vidéos sur YouTube. **Ma sœur** se lève à 7:15 et s'habille à 7:30. Ensuite, elle va à l'université à 8:15. Elle étudie les sciences. À midi, elle va au gymnase. Après, à 3 heures, elle va a son cours de biologie. De 6 à 8 heures, elle joue sur son ordinateur et un peu plus tard, à 8:30, elle discute avec son ami Philippe.

 **THE LANGUAGE GYM**

UNIT 17 – DESCRIBING MY HOUSE

1. Multiple choice quiz

		a	b	c
1	**J'habite**	dans une ferme	dans un appartement	**dans une maison**
2	**Mes grands-parents habitent**	**à la montagne**	dans la banlieue	en centre-ville
3	**Mes cousins habitent**	à la campagne	**dans un quartier chic**	en centre-ville
4	**Mon meilleur ami habite**	**près de la plage**	en centre-ville	sur la côte
5	**Ma petite amie habite**	au bord de la mer	**à la campagne**	à la montagne
6	**Mon oncle et ma tante habitent**	dans une maison	**dans une vieille maison**	dans un manoir

TRANSCRIPT:

(1) J'habite dans une maison. (2) Mes grands-parents habitent à la montagne. (3) Mes cousins habitent dans un quartier chic. (4) Mon meilleur ami habite près de la plage. (5) Ma petite amie habite à la campagne. (6) Mon oncle et ma tante habitent dans une vieille maison.

2. Listening slalom: follow the speaker from top to bottom and number the boxes accordingly

1	2	3	4
J'habite dans une grande (1)	J'habite dans un (2)	J'habite dans un petit (3)	Dans ma maison (4)
vieil appartement, (2)	**et jolie maison (1)**	il y a six (4)	chalet (3)
assez chaleureux (3)	pièces. (4)	**dans la banlieue (1)**	mais il est près de (2)
Ma pièce (4)	la côte. (2)	à la montagne. (3)	**de Paris. (1)**
Mon endroit (2)	préférée (4)	**J'adore ma maison (1)**	Ma pièce (3)
préférée est (3)	**car elle est (1)**	préféré, c'est (2)	est (4)
la terrasse. (2)	le salon. (4)	**neuve et moderne. (1)**	ma chambre. (3)

TRANSCRIPT:

(1) **J'habite dans une grande et jolie maison dans la banlieue de Paris. J'adore ma maison, car elle est neuve et moderne.**
(2) J'habite dans un vieil appartement, mais il est près de la côte. Mon endroit préféré, c'est la terrasse.
(3) J'habite dans un petit chalet assez chaleureux à la montagne. Ma pièce préférée est ma chambre.
(4) Dans ma maison, il y a six pièces. Ma pièce préférée est le salon.

3. Spot the differences and correct your text

Je m'appelle Michel et **je suis** de Nernier, près de Genève. J'ai **quatorze** ans. J'ai les cheveux **blonds** et les yeux **verts**. Physiquement, je suis grand et **mince**. De caractère, je suis **bavard** et assez **sympa**. Je m'entends bien avec ma famille, car ils sont tous **aimables**. Ma nourriture préférée, ce sont les fruits ~~de mer~~. J'en mange tous les jours. Je suis très sportif et pendant mon temps libre, j'aime faire du foot**ing**, jouer au tennis, aller au **gymnase** et faire de l'**escalade**. En général, je me **lève** très tôt, vers six heures et je me couche à **minuit**. J'habite dans une **grande** et **vieille** maison dans le centre de Genève, près du **lac**. J'adore ma maison. Ma pièce préférée est le salon, car c'est très **spacieux** et c'est très bien **meublé**.

4. Spot the missing words and write them in

Je m'appelle Fabrizio. Je viens **d'**Italie. J'habite dans **une** grande et jolie maison sur la côte. Chez moi, **il y a** dix pièces et ma pièce favorite, **c'est** la cuisine. J'aime cuisiner dans la **cuisine** avec ma mère. Tous les jours, je **me** lève, je me douche dans la salle **de bain** et ensuite, je **m'**habille dans ma chambre. Je joue souvent **sur** mon ordinateur **dans** le salon. Mon ami Pablo habite dans une **petite** maison à la montagne. C'est une maison très vieille, **mais** très chaleureuse. Pablo est **très** marrant et travailleur. Il n'aime pas **sa** maison, car elle est **trop** petite.

5. Faulty translation: correct the translation

My name is Romain and I am **from** Biarritz, in the Basque country. My **apartment** is **on the outskirts** of the city and I live **near** the coast. At home, I speak Basque and French. Basque is a very beautiful and very **old** language. I live in a big apartment; it is **new** and beautiful. The rooms are very **spacious**. **We have** a huge terrace with a small **swimming pool**. My **rabbit** lives in the garden. Its name is Papinou. My favourite **room** at home, is the **dining room**, because I love eating. I also like relaxing in my **bedroom**. I always watch **cartoons** and series on Netflix. I also do my **homework** there.

TRANSCRIPT:

Je m'appelle Romain et je suis **de** Biarritz, au Pays basque. Mon **appartement** est **dans la banlieue** de la ville et je vis **près de** la côte. Chez moi, je parle basque et français. Le basque est une très jolie et très **ancienne** langue. J'habite dans un grand appartement, il est **neuf** et joli. Les pièces sont très **spacieuses**. **Nous avons** une terrasse énorme avec une petite **piscine**. Mon **lapin** habite dans le jardin. Il s'appelle Papinou. Ma **pièce** favorite chez moi, c'est la **salle à manger**, car j'adore manger. J'aime aussi me détendre dans ma **chambre**. Je regarde toujours des **dessins animés** et des séries sur Netflix. Je fais aussi mes **devoirs** là.

6. Fill in the grid

	Description of house	Favourite part of the house
1	Old	Garden
2	Beautiful	Bathroom
3	New	Living room
4	Ugly	Dining room
5	Small	Own Bedroom
6	Spacious	Game room
7	Modern	Kitchen
8	Big	Terrace

TRANSCRIPT:

1. J'habite dans une vieille maison. Je préfère le jardin.
2. J'habite dans une jolie maison. J'adore la salle de bain.
3. Nous vivons dans une maison neuve. Le salon est ma pièce préférée.
4. J'habite dans une maison très moche. La seule pièce que j'aime, c'est la salle à manger.
5. Nous vivons dans une petite maison. J'adore ma chambre.
6. Nous habitons dans une maison spacieuse. Je préfère la salle de jeux.
7. Nous vivons dans une maison moderne. J'adore la cuisine.
8. Nous habitons dans une grande maison. Pour moi, la terrasse est la meilleure partie de la maison.

7. Gapped sentences: fill in the gaps

a. J'habite dans une grande et **jolie** maison.

b. Ma maison est dans la **banlieue** de Valence.

c. J'ai aussi une maison à la **campagne**.

d. Mon meilleur ami habite dans un appartement très **petit** en **centre-ville**.

e. Ma petite amie habite dans un **petit** appartement dans un quartier **résidentiel** sur la **côte**.

f. Mes grands-parents vivent à la **montagne**.

g. Mon oncle favori, Paul, habite dans un **immeuble** dans le centre-ville de Lyon.

8. Listen, spot and correct the spelling and grammar errors

Je m'appelle Penny. Je suis anglais**e** et je vis dans une vieille **maison** à la campagne, **en** Italie. J'adore ma maison! Chez **moi**, il y a 5 pièces**,** mais ma pièce préféré**e**, c'est le salon. Tous **les** jours, après **le** collège j'aime **me** reposer dans le salon et regarder **la** télé avec ma sœur. Je n'aime pas la salle **de** bain, car parfois, il y a des souris! Nous avons une salle de **jeux** assez grande où mon frère et moi jou**ons** à la Playstation.

9. Complete (in English) with the correct details

	Caroline	Philippe	Jean-Marc
Town	Toulouse (France)	Marrakesh (Maroc)	Dakar (Sénégal)
Description of house (2 details)	Small and old	Beautiful and spacious	New but ugly
Location of house	Outskirts	City-centre	Countryside
Favourite room	Kitchen	Bedroom	Living room
Another room they like	Bedroom	Garden	Game room
Room they hate	Dining room	Living room	Bathroom

TRANSCRIPT:
1. Salut, je suis Caroline! Je suis de Toulouse et j'habite dans une vieille et petite maison dans la banlieue de ma ville. Ma pièce préférée? C'est la cuisine, mais j'aime aussi ma chambre. Cependant, notre salle à manger est très moche. Je la déteste.
2. Salut, je suis Philippe et je suis de Marrakesh, au Maroc. Ma maison est jolie et spacieuse. Je vis en centre-ville. Ma pièce préférée, c'est ma chambre même si le jardin est bien aussi. La pièce que je déteste, c'est le salon. Il est froid, vieux et obscur.
3. Salut, je suis Jean-Marc et je suis de Dakar, au Sénégal. Ma maison est neuve, mais moche. Je vis à la campagne. Ma pièce préférée, c'est le salon et j'aime aussi la salle de jeux. Cependant, notre salle de bain est horrible. Il y a toujours des cafards énormes!

10. Narrow listening: gapped translation

My house is very **small** and cosy. It is situated on the **outskirts** of Cannes, a city in the south of France, on the **coast,** 5 minutes away from the Midi **beach**. I live in a **residential area**. In my house there are six rooms: a kitchen, a toilet, a living room, and three **bedrooms**. My favourite room is the **living room** because it is **comfortable**, well-furnished and beautiful. I also like my bedroom because I have my Playstation and my **computer**. I like **to relax** and do my homework in my bedroom. I hate the **bathroom**, because it is too **small** and old. It also smells very **bad.**

TRANSCRIPT:
Ma maison est très **petite** et chaleureuse. Elle est située dans la **banlieue** de Cannes, une ville dans le sud de la France, sur la **côte,** à 5 minutes de la **plage** du Midi. Je vis dans une **zone résidentielle.** Dans ma maison, il y a six pièces: une cuisine, des toilettes, un salon et trois **chambres**. Ma pièce préférée, c'est **le salon** car c'est **confortable**, bien meublé et joli. J'aime aussi ma chambre, car j'ai ma Playstation et mon **ordinateur**. J'aime **me reposer** et faire mes devoirs dans ma chambre. Je déteste la **salle de bain**, car c'est trop **petit** et vieux et en plus ça sent très **mauvais.**

11. Answer the questions in English

1. How old is Oscar? **14**
2. Where is he from? **France**
3. Where does he live? **Tahiti**
4. What does he look like? (3 details) **Tall, sporty, a bit fat**
5. What is his character like? (3 details) **Sometimes lazy, sometimes hard working, quite funny**
6. What are his favourite clothes? (2 details) **Jeans and a white t-shirt**
7. What's his favourite food? (2) **Salad and seafood soup**
8. At what time does he wake up? **5am**
9. After school he goes for a walk with **his dog** and then he **does his homework.**
10. Does he live in a house or in a flat? **A flat**
11. What is his house/flat like? (2) **Small but comfortable**
12. What is his favourite room? **The kitchen**
13. What is the room he hates the most? **His bedroom**
14. What does he say about his bedroom? (2 details) **It's too small, there's no WIFI**

11. TRANSCRIPT:
Salut, je suis Oscar et j'ai 14 ans. Je suis de France, mais maintenant je vis à Tahiti avec ma famille. Je suis grand et sportif, mais un peu gros. De caractère, parfois je suis paresseux, parfois je suis travailleur, et je suis aussi assez marrant. Je porte presque toujours un jean et une chemise blanche. J'adore ça! Ma nourriture préférée, c'est la salade et la soupe de fruits de mer. Le matin, je me lève à 5 heures. Après le collège, je sors faire une promenade avec mon chien et je fais aussi mes devoirs. J'habite dans un appartement et il est petit, mais confortable. Ma pièce préférée, c'est la cuisine car il y a toujours de la nourriture. Cependant, je déteste ma chambre car c'est trop petit et il n'y a pas de wifi.

UNIT 18 – SAYING WHAT I DO AT HOME / DAILY ROUTINE

1. Mosaic listening: follow the speaker from <u>left</u> to <u>right</u> and number accordingly

1	**Vers sept heures (1)**	je prépare le repas (5)	et je joue sur mon ordinateur (4)	dans ma chambre (2)
2	En général (2)	**je prends mon petit-déjeuner (1)**	des films (3)	dans la salle de jeux (4)
3	Quand j'ai le temps (3)	j'écoute de la musique et (2)	**dans la cuisine (1)**	dans le salon (3)
4	Souvent (4)	j'aide (6)	avec ma mère (5)	**avec mes frères (1)**
5	Parfois (5)	je surfe sur internet (4)	je fais mes devoirs (2)	dans le jardin (6)
6	Tous les week-ends (6)	je regarde (3)	mon père (6)	dans la cuisine (5)

TRANSCRIPT:

1. **Vers sept heures, je prends mon petit-déjeuner dans la cuisine avec mes frères**.
2. En général, j'écoute de la musique et je fais mes devoirs dans ma chambre.
3. Quand j'ai le temps, je regarde des films dans le salon.
4. Souvent, je surfe sur internet et je joue sur mon ordinateur dans la salle de jeux.
5. Parfois, je prépare le repas avec ma mère dans la cuisine.
6. Tous les week-ends, j'aide mon père dans le jardin.

2. Listen and fill in the gaps

a. Souvent, je **discute** avec ma mère dans la cuisine.

b. De temps en temps, je joue à la Playstation dans la salle de **jeux**.

c. Deux fois par semaine, je **fais** du vélo.

d. Souvent, je prépare le repas dans la **cuisine**.

e. Je fais toujours mes devoirs dans le **salon**.

f. En général, je me douche dans la **salle** de bain de mes parents.

g. Quand il fait beau, je **lis** des magazines dans le jardin.

h. Je ne **regarde** jamais la télé dans le salon avec mes parents.

3. Break the flow

a. Je ne regarde jamais la télé dans le salon avec mes parents.

b. En général, je range mon vélo dans le garage.

c. Tous les jours, je poste des photos sur Instagram.

d. Une ou deux fois par semaine, je prépare le repas dans la cuisine.

e. Je ne prends jamais mon petit-déjeuner avec mes frères dans la salle à manger.

f. En général, après le collège je regarde la télé dans ma chambre.

4. Faulty translation: what, how often, where? Listen and correct the errors

	What do they do?	How often?	Where?
1	Chats with his mother	**often**	**in the kitchen**
2	Helps father	once a week	**in the garden**
3	**Plays on Playstation**	every day	**in the game room**
4	Does homework	**three** times a week	in the living room
5	Goes on the internet	often	in his **brother's** room
6	**Has lunch**	every day	in the dining room
7	Prepares food	**always**	in the kitchen
8	Rides his bike	**normally**	**in the garden**

TRANSCRIPT:

1. Salut, je suis Georges. Je discute souvent avec ma mère dans la cuisine.
2. J'aide mon père une fois par semaine dans le jardin.
3. Je joue à la Playstation tous les jours dans la salle de jeux.
4. Je fais mes devoirs trois fois par semaine dans le salon.
5. Je vais souvent sur internet dans la chambre de mon frère.
6. Je déjeune tous les jours dans la salle à manger.
7. Je prépare toujours le repas dans la cuisine.
8. Normalement, je fais du vélo dans le jardin.

5. Likely or Unlikely? Write "L" or "U" for each sentence you hear and then explain why

1	U	Je me douche dans la cuisine.
2	L	Je regarde la télé dans ma chambre.
3	L	Je déjeune dans la salle à manger.
4	U	Je prépare le repas dans la salle à manger.
5	L	Je range mon vélo dans le garage.
6	L	Je fais mes devoirs dans le salon.
7	U	Je me brosse les dents dans la chambre de mes parents.
8	U	Je fais du vélo dans la douche.

6. List the activities in the correct order in which Philippe does them

5	I do my homework
6	I go on the internet
7	I listen to music
1	**I have breakfast**
2	I read my favourite magazines
4	I leave the house
8	I watch a movie
3	I brush my teeth
9	I rest in my bed

TRANSCRIPT:

1. Premièrement, je prends mon petit-déjeuner.
2. Ensuite, je lis mes magazines favoris.
3. Après, je me brosse les dents.
4. Je sors de chez moi à 8 heures.
5. Je fais mes devoirs dans ma chambre.
6. Je vais sur internet pendant une heure.
7. J'écoute de la musique dans le salon.
8. Je regarde un film avec mon frère.
9. Finalement, je me repose dans mon lit.

7. Listen to the verbs and add them in where appropriate

a. Je **discute** avec ma mère.

b. Je **vais** sur internet.

c. Je **prépare** le repas.

d. Je **fais** mes devoirs.

e. Je **me brosse** les dents.

f. Je **mange** des céréales.

g. Je **poste** des photos sur Instagram.

h. Je **regarde** des films.

 **THE LANGUAGE GYM**

8. Narrow listening: gapped translation

Every day, I get up at five in the morning. Then I **shower** and I have breakfast in the **kitchen**. After that, I brush my teeth and I **prepare** my **bag**. Then, I **get dressed** and I go to school at **7:30**. Normally, I go by **bike**. When I **return home**, I chat on Skype with my family in Australia and I go on the internet in my **bedroom**. Then, I **cycle** in the garden with my two **dogs**. Sometimes, I watch **cartoons** and I post photos on Instagram in **my brother's room**. Usually, I have dinner at around **8**. After dinner, I **watch movies** and then I shower. Finally, I read my favourite **comics** and I go to bed at **midnight**.

TRANSCRIPT:
Tous les jours, je me lève à cinq heures du matin. Ensuite, **je me douche** et je prends mon petit-déjeuner dans la **cuisine**. Après cela, je me brosse les dents et je prépare mon **sac**. Ensuite, **je m'habille** et je vais au collège à **7:30**. Normalement, j'y vais en **vélo**. Quand je **rentre à la maison**, je tchatte sur Skype avec ma famille en Australie et je vais sur internet dans ma **chambre**. Après, **je fais du vélo** dans le jardin avec mes deux **chiens**. Parfois, je regarde des **dessins animés** et je poste des photos sur Instagram dans **la chambre de mon frère**. D'habitude, je dîne vers **8** heures. Après le dîner, je **regarde des films** et ensuite je me douche. Finalement, je lis mes **bandes dessinées** favorites et je me couche à **minuit**.

9. Sentence puzzle: listen and rewrite correctly

1. Je me réveille toujours tôt, vers six heures moins dix.

2. Pour le petit-déjeuner, je mange seulement un œuf et deux tartines avec de la confiture.

3. Je sors de chez moi à sept heures moins le quart et je vais au collège en vélo.

4. J'ai un frère qui s'appelle Joël et il est très paresseux et antipathique.

5. Tous les jours, je fais du vélo dans le jardin avec mes deux chiens.

6. En général, après le dîner, je regarde la télé dans le salon avec mes parents ou seul.

10. Answer the questions about Marie

1. At what time does she always get up during the week?
6:45
2. How does she go to school?
On foot
3. What is her favourite school subject?
French
4. What two sports does she do after school?
Basketball / Weight lifting
5. Where does she normally chat with her mother?
On the terrace or in the kitchen
6. In which room does she do her homework?
The living room
7. What does she never do during dinner?
Watches TV with her parents
8. What three things does she do after dinner?
Reads comics, chats on Skype, watches videos on YouTube
9. What two things does she do before going to bed?
Showers and brushes her teeth
10. At what time does she go to bed?
Midnight

10. Answer the questions about Marie

TRANSCRIPT:

Salut, je suis Marie et j'ai 15 ans. Pendant la semaine, je me lève toujours à 6:45. Ensuite, je vais au collège à pied avec mon frère. Ma matière préférée, c'est le français car c'est divertissant, facile et utile pour le futur. Après le collège, je joue au basket et je fais de la musculation au gymnase. Quand je rentre chez moi, normalement je discute avec ma mère, parfois sur la terrasse et parfois dans la cuisine. Je fais mes devoirs dans le salon tous les jours. Quand je dîne, je ne regarde jamais la télé avec mes parents, car ils regardent des séries très ennuyeuses. Après le dîner, je lis des bandes dessinées, je tchatte sur Skype et je regarde des vidéos sur YouTube. Avant de me coucher, je me douche et je me brossse les dents. Je me couche à minuit. Au revoir!

UNIT 19 – TALKING ABOUT FUTURE PLANS AND HOLIDAYS

1. Listen and fill in the gaps

1. Cet été, je **vais** aller en vacances en Corse.

2. Je vais voyager en **avion**.

3. Nous allons **passer** une semaine là-bas.

4. Ce **sera** divertissant.

5. Je vais **rester** dans un hôtel de luxe.

6. Je vais **danser**.

7. Nous allons faire les **magasins**.

8. J'aimerais faire de la **plongée**.

9. Nous aimerions **faire** du sport.

2. Spot the differences and correct your text

a. Cet **été**, je vais aller en vacances au Maroc.

b. Je vais passer **deux semaines** là-bas.

c. Je vais y aller avec **ma petite amie**.

d. Nous allons rester dans un hôtel **bon marché**.

e. Je vais faire du **sport**.

f. Mon **frère** va acheter des **vêtements**.

g. Nous allons aller à la **plage**.

h. Je vais **bronzer** au soleil.

i. J'aimerais faire de la **plongée**.

j. Nous aimerions **faire les magasins**.

3. Listen and tick the correct details

Paul	**va aller au Japon** ✓
	va voyager en bateau
	va rester dans un hôtel de luxe ✓
	va manger beaucoup de sushis ✓
	va aller en boîte
Anne	va aller en Italie
	va voyager en train ✓
	va rester dans un camping
	va faire du tourisme
	va manger beaucoup de pâtes ✓
Carole	va aller en France
	va voyager en vélo
	va rester dans une auberge de jeunesse ✓
	va aller à la plage
	va visiter des sites historiques ✓
Céline	**va aller en Grèce** ✓
	va voyager en avion et en bateau
	va faire de la plongée
	va faire du tourisme ✓
	va manger beaucoup de salades niçoises ✓

4. Write in the missing words

Cet été, je vais aller en vacances **à** Rome, **en** Italie. Je **vais** voyager en avion. Nous allons passer une semaine **là-bas**. Nous allons **rester** dans un hôtel **de** luxe. **Je** vais aller en boîte. Mes sœurs vont aller faire **les** magasins et mes parents vont **aller** acheter des souvenirs et faire du tourisme car **il y a** beaucoup de sites historiques **ici**.

5. Guess what comes next then listen to see how many you guessed right

a. Je vais aller en vacances en **bateau**.

b. Je vais passer **cinq** jours là-bas.

c. Je vais rester dans un **hôtel**.

d. Le matin, je vais aller **à la plage**.

e. L'après-midi, je vais faire du **tourisme**.

f. Le soir, je vais aller **en boîte**.

6. Multiple choice quiz

	a	b	c
1	He is Swiss	He is Swedish	He is Russian
2	He is travelling by train	He is travelling by plane	**He is travelling by boat**
3	**He is travelling alone**	He is travelling with his friend	He is travelling with his family
4	He is going to stay in a cheap hotel	He is going to stay in a three-star hotel	**He is going to stay in a luxury hotel**
5	**He is going to stay there for 2 weeks**	He is going to stay there for 3 weeks	He is going to stay there for 10 days
6	He is going to scuba dive	**He is going to go clubbing**	He is going to eat and sleep
7	He is also going to go sightseeing	He is also going to go shopping	**He is also going to sunbathe**
8	It will be fun	**It will be great**	It will be expensive

TRANSCRIPT: **(1)** Il est suisse. **(2)** Il voyage en bateau. **(3)** Il voyage seul. **(4)** Il va rester dans un hôtel de luxe. **(5)** Il va passer deux semaines là-bas. **(6)** Il va aller en boîte. **(7)** Il va aussi bronzer au soleil. **(8)** Ce sera génial!

7. Faulty translation: spot the translation errors and correct them

This **summer,** I am going to go on holiday to Reunion Island. I am going to travel by **plane**. I am going to go there with my **family**. We are going to spend ten **days** there. We are going to stay in a good hotel in Saint-Denis, the capital of Reunion Island. It is a very **beautiful** place with a lively nightlife. There are lots of **beaches** and our hotel is **near** the sea. Every day, I am going to go to the beach. In the morning, I am going to swim and **scuba dive**. I am also going to **sunbathe**. In the afternoon, we are going to go **sightseeing**. My parents are going to buy **souvenirs** and my sister is going to **read** lots of books, as always. For dinner, we will go to **local** restaurants. We will eat a lot of **fish** and **seafood**.

TRANSCRIPT: Cet **été**, je vais aller en vacances à l'île de La Réunion. Je vais voyager en **avion**. Je vais y aller avec ma **famille**. Nous allons y passer dix **jours**. Nous allons loger dans un bon hôtel à Saint-Denis, la capitale de l'île de La Réunion. C'est un lieu très **beau** avec une vie nocturne animée. Il y a beaucoup de **plages** et notre hôtel est **près de** la mer. Tous les jours, je vais aller à la plage. Le matin, je vais nager et **faire de la plongée**. Je vais aussi **bronzer au soleil**. L'après-midi, nous allons **faire du tourisme**. Mes parents vont acheter des **souvenirs** et ma sœur va **lire** beaucoup de livres, comme toujours. Pour le dîner, nous irons dans des restaurants **locaux**. Nous mangerons beaucoup de **poisson** et de **fruits de mer**.

8. Listen, spot and correct the spelling and grammar errors

Cet été, je vais aller **en** vacances **en** avion en Allemagne. Je vais **passer** deux semaines là-bas. Je vais y aller avec toute **ma** famille. Nous allons rest**er** dans un hôtel de **luxe** avec une piscine près de la **rivière**. Le matin, nous allons aller à la **pêche**. L'après-midi, nous allons faire **les** magasins et faire du tourisme. Vers huit heures, **nous** allons dîner dans un **restaurant** local pour manger des plats **typiques**. Le soir, ma sœur et moi **allons** aller en boîte. J'aime**rais** aussi visiter Berlin. Ce **sera** génial!

9. Complete in English with the correct details

Holiday destination	Mauritius, Indian Ocean
Means of transport	Plane
Duration	12 days
Who with	Her boyfriend
Accomodation	A luxury hotel
Activities	1. Rest
	2. Scuba diving
	3. Clubbing

9. Transcript

Pour les prochaines vacances d'été, je vais aller à l'île Maurice, dans l'océan indien. Je vais voyager en avion et je vais passer 12 jours là-bas avec mon petit ami. Nous allons rester un hôtel de luxe. Pendant les vacances, je veux faire 3 choses: je veux me reposer, faire de la plongée, et je voudrais aussi aller en boîte le soir.

10. Listen and arrange the information in the same order as it occurs in the text

1	My name is Gabrièle
4	We are going to stay there nine days
2	This summer I am going to go on holiday to Corsica
7	The hotel is near the beach
9	We are going to sunbathe
5	We are going to travel by boat
8	We are going to go to the beach every day
6	We are going to stay in a four-star hotel
12	We are going back home on 13th July
10	We are going to scuba dive
3	I am going to go with my best friends
11	At night we are going to go clubbing

TRANSCRIPT: (1) Je m'appelle Gabrièle.
(2) Cet été, je vais aller en vacances en Corse.
(3) Je vais y aller avec mes meilleures amies.
(4) Nous allons y passer 9 jours. (5) Nous allons voyager en bateau. (6) Nous allons rester dans un hôtel 4 étoiles. (7) L'hôtel est près de la plage.
(8) Nous allons aller à la plage tous les jours. (9) Nous allons bronzer au soleil. (10) Nous allons faire de la plongée (11) Le soir, nous allons aller en boîte. (12) Nous allons rentrer à la maison le 13 juillet.

11. Listen to Charles and answer the questions below in English

1. In which part of France is he going on holiday?
In the southwest
2. When does his holiday begin? **On the 20th June**
3. How long for? **Two weeks**
4. How is he travelling? **Car**
5. Who with? **His best friend**
6. Who are they staying with? **With his cousin**
7. In which part of town are they going to stay?
On the outskits, on the coast, 10 minutes away from the city centre
8. What activities are they going to do? (4 details)
**a. Go to the beach   b. Sunbathe
c. Eat local food   d. Do (a bit of) sightseeing**

TRANSCRIPT:
Salut, je suis Charles. Cet été, je vais aller en vacances à Hendaye, dans le sud-ouest de la France. Mes vacances commencent le 20 juin. Je vais passer deux semaines là-bas et je vais voyager en voiture, avec mon meilleur ami. Nous allons rester chez mon cousin. Il habite dans la banlieue de la ville. C'est situé sur la côte, à 10 minutes du centre-ville. Comme activités, nous allons aller à la plage, bronzer au soleil, manger de la nourriture locale et faire un peu de tourisme.

12. Narrow listening: fill in the grid

	Caroline	Benjamin	Sophie	Mathieu
Who with	Boyfriend	Family	Three friends	Best friend
Destination	South of France	Northern Italy	South of Spain	Japan
Departure date	20th May	1st July	15th August	30th September
How long for	1 month	2 weeks	5 days	1 week
Accommodation	A friend's house	Farm	Luxury hotel	Cheap hotel
Location	Mountain	Countryside	Coast	City centre
Activities	1. Cycling 2. Climbing 3. Eating and sleeping	1. Resting 2. Hiking 3. Horse riding	1. Swimming 2. Scuba diving 3. Sunbathing	1. Sightseeing 2. Shopping 3. Clubbing

TRANSCRIPT:
(1) Salut, je suis **Caroline**. Cet été, je vais aller en vacances avec mon petit ami dans le sud de la France. Nous allons partir le 20 mai et nous allons passer un mois là-bas. Nous allons rester chez une amie. Notre amie habite à la montagne. Pendant les vacances, nous allons faire du vélo, de l'escalade et nous allons dormir et manger beaucoup.
(2) Salut, je suis **Benjamin**. Cet été, je vais aller en vacances avec ma famille dans le nord de l'Italie. Nous allons partir le premier juillet et nous allons passer deux semaines là-bas. Nous allons rester dans une ferme à la campagne. Pendant les vacances, nous allons nous reposer, faire de la randonnée et faire de l'équitation. J'adore les chevaux!
(3) Salut, je m'appelle **Sophie**. Cet été, je vais aller en vacances avec trois amies dans le sud de l'Espagne. Nous allons partir le 15 août et nous allons passer 5 jours là-bas. Nous allons rester dans un hôtel de luxe. L'hôtel est sur la côte. Pendant les vacances, nous allons nager, faire de la plongée et bronzer au soleil.
(4) Salut, je suis **Mathieu**. Cet été, je vais aller en vacances avec mon meilleur ami au Japon. Nous allons partir le 30 septembre et nous allons passer une semaine là-bas. Nous allons rester dans un hôtel bon marché en centre-ville. Pendant les vacances nous allons faire du tourisme, faire les magasins et aussi aller en boîte.

Printed in Great Britain
by Amazon

49852183R00037